Beginnings
of the
Prose Poem:

ALL OVER THE PLACE

Beginnings
of the
Prose Poem:

ALL OVER THE PLACE

Mary Ann Caws and Michel Delville, eds.

BLACK
WIDOW
PRESS

Joseph S. Phillips and Susan J. Wood, Ph.D., Publishers
www.blackwidowpress.com

Cover Art: William Blake, *Jerusalem*, Plate 1, Frontispiece, created 1804–1820.

Design, Typesetting & Production: Kerrie Kemperman

ISBN-13: 978-1-7338924-7-6

Printed in the United States
10 9 8 7 6 5 4 3 2 1

The editors extend their gratitude to Joe Phillips at Black Widow Press for his support and unflinching enthusiasm for this project. Special thanks are due to Kerrie Kemperman for the splendid design. We want especially to thank all our translators, whose generosity in giving their time and talents to this enterprise was above all the priceless enabling factor and they of course retain their rights to their translations. Thanks are also due to Shuyu Guo for the Chinese characters accompanying the Segalen poems. This book was published with the help of the UR Traverses, ULiège Belgium.

Table of Contents

Introduction

Mary Ann Caws and Michel Delville

With its very title and its form based on contradiction, the prose poem is suitable to an extraordinary range of perception and expression, from the ambivalent (in content as in form) to the mimetic and the narrative (or even anecdotal). It has been suggested that the prose poem, like its not-so-distant cousin, free verse, was born in France out of a sense of frustration with the strict rules of 18th-century French neoclassicism. If so, these rules are to be thanked since the prose poem occasions even now a rapidly increasing interest. For the vast majority of poets and critics, its principal characteristics are those that would insure unity even in epiphanic brevity and poetic quality even without the line breaks of free verse: high patterning, rhythmic and figural repetition, sustained intensity, and compactness.[1]

For Jonathan Monroe the prose poem operates as a "heteroglot"[2] genre in the Bakhtinian sense, its rejection of the personal voice mode and its tendency to represent a variety of private and public discourses such as Charles Baudelaire's dialogues between rich and poor, the transdiscursive textures of Arthur Rimbaud's *Illuminations,* or Amy Lowell's polyphonic prose. The foundational models represented by Baudelaire and Rimbaud are all represented here, alongside lesser-known French and non-French examples which suggest that the prose poem began much earlier than with Baudelaire's celebrated *Paris Spleen.* Whereas Monroe's model is predominantly Romantic (Schlegel's theory of a progressive *Universalpoesie* anticipates the fusion of genres articulated by the prose poem), Peter Dronke[3] and Nathalie Dauvois have gone back further into time and considered the Renaissance *prosimètre* (a prose-poetry hybrid which gained popularity as a pastoral genre in the Renaissance) as a possible precedent. Fabienne Moore has identified the prose poem as one of the Enlightenment's best kept secrets, while others have turned to the prose versets of the Bible, to classical and folk lyrics, to the poeticized prose of such romantics as Chateaubriand, to the intermixtures of verse and prose in Samuel Taylor Coleridge's notebooks, to Maurice de Guérin's emblematic "Le Centaure," to Ivan Turgenev's object poems, and of course to Aloysius Bertrand's *Gaspard de la nuit,* most of whom represented here side by side with more unusual suspects such as Friedrich Hölderlin, Frans Erens, Judith Gautier, Masaoka Shiki and Lu Xun—the last three reminding us in passing that the rich histories and legacies of the Japanese and Chinese prose poem have largely been ignored even by specialists of the genre.

The sheer diversity of writers appearing in this anthology showcases the richness and variety of a tradition marked as much by Blake's visionary mysticism as by Wilde's Decadentism, Gertrude Stein's Cubism and Mina Loy's irresistibly zany Futuristic eccentricities. Luckily, many of the poems featured here cannot be contained within a single formal or generic category. Whereas some aspire to the condition of lyric, narrative or expository prose, many resist classification while others, like Joyce, Fillìa, Jacob or Nougé, tend toward the unfinished, the fragmentary or the aphoristic. That said, readers looking for patterns of continuity and influence will recognize the emergence and development of certain broad trends which are still very much alive in the recent and current evolution of the genre. Among these recurrent trends and subgenres, the dreamscape (favored by Lord Dunsany, Eugene Jolas and Harry Crosby) and the fable stand out, the latter being practiced, often in a subversive, when not absurdist fashion, by such antithetical poets as Wilde, Elena Guro or Daniil Kharms, before it became one of the hallmarks of the contemporary American prose poem in the hands of Russell Edson, Lydia Davis, Maxine Chernoff and others.

Formal and terminological considerations aside, it is the strong connection between the genre and the visual arts which was to dominate the development of the prose poem until today, beginning with Blake's picture-poems and Bertrand's *Gaspard de la nuit*—the main inspiration behind Baudelaire's *petits poèmes en prose*—which was intended as a tribute to Rembrandt's and Callot's 17th century grotesques. Many of our prose poems here, from early to more recent, use the visual to enhance the verbal and vice versa: Bertrand's "Haarlem" starts us off there, and Stein's *Tender Buttons* lead us on there, as do Huysmans and some others we have chosen. The ekphrastic quality of the eighteenth, nineteenth and early twentieth century prose poetry can be traced back to a number of short descriptive prose genres, including the portrait, the *blason,* the Rousseau-esque *rêverie* or even the *salon,* a genre of lyrical writing about works of art, which John Simon sees as the main impulse behind Bertrand's prose poems.[4] The close connection between the prose poem and verbovisual art remained evident in Rimbaud's choice of the title *Illuminations* for his second collection of prose poems, as well as in Baudelaire's intention to modernize the method Bertrand applied to "the old days, so strangely picturesque." In the modernist period, which concludes this volume, the influence of impressionism and cubism, in particular, proved seminal in the development of a modernist aesthetic and ethos of the prose poem as the examples of Virginia Woolf, Max Jacob, Pierre Reverdy and others indicate.

We are hoping that the readers of this anthology will both encounter something new, and feel inspired to remember other texts admired and loved, perhaps more poetically than prosaically. Even as the prose poem occupies a controversial space, hovering between genres, its reach is vast, as is the selection here from Blake in the late 18th century to Kharms in the 1920s. The multiply diverse tones range from the ironic and sharp-witted to a lyric flow, and the poets, from the more familiar to the less so, from the occidental to the oriental, from the expected, like the cubist prose poets Jacob and Reverdy, and from the well-known writers, like Colette, Wilde, Rilke, and Kafka, to the less expected: novelists like Joyce and Woolf, and the lesser-known in a joyous mixture of voices.

---

[1] The editors of this volume subscribe to this view; hence their decision not to include sections from longer prose poetry sequences such as Lautréamont's *Les Chants de Maldoror* or William Carlos Williams' *Kora in Hell.*

[2] Jonathan Monroe, *A Poverty of Objects: The Prose Poem and the Politics of Genre* (Ithaca: Cornell University Press, 1987), 33..

[3] Peter Dronke, *Verse With Prose from Petronius to Dante: The Art and Scope of the Mixed Form* (Cambridge: Harvard University Press, 1994), 2.

[4] John Simon, *The Prose Poem as a Genre in Nineteenth-Century European Literature* (New York, Garland press, 1987), 96.

William Blake

A Memorable Fancy

An Angel came to me and said O pitiable foolish young man! O horrible! O dreadful state! consider the hot burning dungeon thou art preparing for thyself to all eternity, to which thou art going in such career.

I said, perhaps you will be willing to shew me my eternal lot & we will contemplate together upon it and see whether your lot or mine is most desirable.

So he took me thro' a stable & thro' a church & down into the church vault at the end of which was a mill: thro' the mill we went, and came to a cave, down the winding cavern we groped our tedious way till a void boundless as a nether sky appear'd beneath us, & we held by the roots of trees and hung over this immensity, but I said, if you please we will commit ourselves to this void, and see whether providence is here also, if you will not, I will? but he answer'd, do not presume O young-man but as we here remain behold thy lot which will soon appear when the darkness passes away.

So I remain'd with him sitting in the twisted root of an oak; he was suspended in a fungus, which hung with the head downward into the deep.

By degrees we beheld the infinite Abyss, fiery as the smoke of a burning city; beneath us at an immense distance was the sun, black but shining; round it were fiery tracks on which revolv'd vast spiders, crawling after their prey; which flew or rather swum in the infinite deep, in the most terrific shapes of animals sprung from corruption, & the air was full of them, & seem'd composed of them; these are Devils, and arc called Powers of the air. I now asked my companion which was my eternal lot? he said, between the black & white spiders.

But now, from between the black & white spiders, a cloud and fire burst and rolled thro' the deep, blackning all beneath, so that the nether deep grew black as a sea & rolled with a terrible noise; beneath us was nothing now to be seen but a black tempest, till looking east between the clouds & the waves, we saw a cataract of blood mixed with fire, and not many stones throw from us appear'd and sunk again the scaly fold of a monstrous serpent; at last to the east, distant about three degrees appear'd a fiery crest above the waves; slowly it reared like a ridge of golden rocks till we discover'd two globes of crimson fire, from which the sea fled away in clouds of smoke, and now we saw, it was the head of Leviathan; his forehead was divided into streaks of green & purple like those on a tygers forehead: soon we saw his mouth & red gills hang just above the raging foam tinging the black deep with beams of blood, advancing toward us with all the fury of a spiritual existence.

My friend the Angel climb'd up from his station into the mill; I remain'd alone, & then this appearance was no more, but I found myself sitting on a pleasant bank beside a river by moonlight hearing a harper who sung to the harp, & his theme was, The man who never alters his opinion is like standing water, & breeds reptiles of the mind.

But I arose, and sought for the mill & there I found my Angel, who surprised asked me how I escaped?

I answer'd, All that we saw was owing to your metaphysics; for when you ran away, I found myself on a bank by moonlight hearing a harper. But now we have seen my eternal lot, shall I shew you yours? he laugh'd at my proposal; but I by force suddenly caught him in my arms, & flew westerly thro' the night, till we were elevated above the earths shadow; then I flung myself with him directly into the body of the sun; here I clothed myself in white, & taking in my hand Sweden-borgs volumes, sunk from the glorious clime, and passed all the planets till we came to saturn; here I staid to rest, & then leap'd into the void, between saturn & the fixed stars.

Here, said I! is your lot, in this space, if space it may be call'd. Soon we saw the stable and the church, & I took him to the altar and open'd the Bible, and lo! it was a deep pit, into which I descended driving the Angel before me; soon we saw seven houses of brick; one we enter'd; in it were a number of monkeys, baboons, & all of that species, chain'd by the middle, grinning and snatching at one another, but witheld by the shortness of their chains; however I saw that they sometimes grew numerous, and then the weak were caught by the strong, and with a grinning aspect, first coupled with & then devour'd, by plucking off first one limb and then another till the body was left a helpless trunk; this after grinning & kissing it with seeming fondness they devour'd too; and here & there I saw one savourily picking the flesh off of his own tail; as the stench terribly annoy'd us both we went into the mill, & I in my hand brought the skeleton of a body, which in the mill was Aristotle's Analytics.

So the Angel said: thy phantasy has imposed upon me & thou oughtest to be ashamed.

I answer'd: we impose on one another, & it is but lost time to converse with you whose works are only Analytics.

Opposition is true Friendship.

I have always found that Angels have the vanity to speak of themselves as the only wise; this they do with a confident insolence sprouting from systematic reasoning:

Thus Swedenborg boasts that what he writes is new; tho' it is only the Contents or Index of already publish'd books.

A man carried a monkey about for a shew, & because he was a little wiser than the monkey, grew vain, and conciev'd himself as much wiser than seven men. It is so with Swedenborg; he shews the folly of churches & exposes hypocrites, till he imagines that all are religious, & himself the single one on earth that ever broke a net.

Now hear a plain fact: Swedenborg has not written one new truth:
Now hear another: he has written all the old falshoods.

And now hear the reason. He conversed with Angels who are all reli-
gious, & conversed not with Devils who all hate religion, for he was
incapable thro' his conceited notions.

Thus Swedenborgs writings are a recapitulation of all superficial,
opinions, and an analysis of the more sublime, but no further.

Have now another plain fact: Any man of mechanical talents may
from the writings of Paracelsus or Jacob Behmen, produce ten
thousand volumes of equal value with Swedenborgs, and from those
of Dante or Shakespeare, an infinite number.

But when he has done this, let him not say that he knows better than
his master, for he only holds a candle in sunshine.

Friedrich Hölderlin

In Lovely Blue
— *translated by Richard Sieburth*

In lovely blue the steeple blossoms from metal roof. Around which
drift swallow cries, around which lies the most moving blue. The sun,
high overhead, tinges the tin of the roof, but up in the wind, silent, the
weathercock crows. When someone takes the stairs down from the bel-
fry, it is a still life, for with the figure thus detached, the sculpted shape
of man steps forth. The windows the bells ring through are as gates to
beauty. Because the gates still take after nature, resembling forest trees.
But purity is also beauty. A grave spirit arises from within, out of
diverse things. Yet so simple these images, so very holy, that one often
truly fears to describe them. But the gods, ever kind, ever immediate,
are rich with virtue and joy. Which man may imitate. May a man look
up from the utter hardship of his life and say: Let me also be like these?
Yes. As long as kindness persists, pure, within his heart, he may be
blessed to measure himself against the divine. Is God unknown? Is he
manifest as the sky? This I tend to believe. Such is man's measure. Well
deserving, yet poetically man dwells on this earth. But the shadow of
the starry night is no more pure, if I may say so, than man, said to be
the image of God.

Is there measure on earth? There is none. For no world of the Cre-
ator ever hindered the course of thunder. A flower is likewise lovely,
blooming as it does under the sun. The eye often discovers creatures
in life it would be yet lovelier to name than flowers. O, this I know!
For to bleed both in body and heart and cease to be whole, is this
pleasing to God? But the soul, I believe, must remain pure, lest the
eagle wing its way up to the Almighty with songs of praise and the
voice of so many birds. A question of substance, and of form. Lovely
little brook, how moving you seem as you roll so clear, like the eye of
God, through the Milky Way. I know you well, but tears pour from
the eye. I see the gaiety of life blossom about me in all of Creation's
forms, because I do not compare it cheaply to the graveyard's solitary

doves. Peoples' laughter seems to grieve me, after all I have a heart. Would I like to be a comet? I think so. They are swift as birds, they flower with fire, childlike in purity. To desire more than this is beyond human measure. The gaiety of virtue also deserves praise from the grave spirit adrift between the garden's three columns. A beautiful virgin should wreathe her hair with myrtle, being simple by nature and heart. But myrtles are found in Greece.

If a man look into a mirror and see his image therein, as if painted, it is his likeness. Man's image has eyes, but the moon has light. King Oedipus may have an eye too many. The sufferings of this man seem indescribable, inexpressible, unspeakable. Which comes when drama represents such things. But what do I feel, now thinking of you? Like brooks, I am carried away by the end of something that expands like Asia. Of course, Oedipus suffers this same? For a reason, of course. Did Hercules suffer as well? Indeed. In their friendship did not the Dioscuri also suffer? Yes, to battle God as Hercules did is to suffer. And to half share immortality with the envy of this life, this too is pain. But this also is suffering, when a man is covered with summer freckles, all bespattered with spots. This is the work of the sun, it draws everything out. It leads young men along their course, charmed by rays like roses. The sufferings of Oedipus seem like a poor man lamenting what he lacks. Son of Laios, poor stranger in Greece. Life is death, and death a life.

Samuel Taylor Coleridge

From *Anima Poetae*

What a swarm of thoughts and feelings, endlessly minute fragments, and, as it were, representations of all preceding and embryos of all future thought, lie compact in any one moment! So, in a single drop of water, the microscope discovers what motions, what tumult, what wars, what pursuits, what stratagems, what a circle-dance of death and life, death-hunting life, and life renewed and invigorated by death! The whole world seems here in a many-meaning cypher. What if our existence was but that moment? What an unintelligible, affrightful riddle, what a chaos of limbs and trunk, tailless, headless, nothing begun and nothing ended, would it not be? And yet scarcely more than that other moment of fifty or sixty years, were that our all? Each part throughout infinite diminution adapted to some other, and yet the whole a means to nothing—ends everywhere, and yet an end nowhere.

★

The love of Nature is ever returned double to us, not only the delighter in our delight, but by linking our sweetest, but of themselves perishable feelings to distinct and vivid images, which we ourselves, at times, and which a thousand casual recollections, recall to our memory. She is the preserver, the treasurer of our joys. Even in sickness and nervous diseases, she has peopled our imagination with lovely forms which have sometimes overpowered the inward pain and brought with them their old sensations. And even when all men have seemed to desert us and the friend of our heart has passed on, with one glance from his "cold disliking eye"—yet even then the blue heaven spreads it out and bends over us, and the little tree still shelters us under its plumage as a second cope, a domestic firmament, and the low creeping gale will sigh in the heath-plant and soothe us by sound of sympathy till the lulled grief lose itself in fixed gaze on the purple heath-blossom, till the present beauty becomes a vision of memory.

★

The humming-moth with its glimmer-mist of rapid unceasing motion before the humble-bee within the flowering bells and cups—and the eagle level with the clouds, himself a cloudy speck, surveys the vale from mount to mount. From the cataract flung on the vale, the broadest fleeces of the snowy foam light on the bank flowers or the water-lilies in the stiller pool below.

Aloysius Bertrand

Haarlem
— *translated by Gian Lombardo*

> When Amsterdam's golden cock sings,
> Haarlem's golden hen lays an egg.
> *The Centuries*, Nostradamus

Haarlem, that marvellous *grotesquerie* epitomizing the Flemish school. Haarlem as painted by Jan Brueghel, Peeter Neef, David Téniers and Paul Rembrandt.

Where blue water ripples in its canals, and where church windows glaze almost golden. Where linen dangles from stone balconies, drying in the sun, and roofs everywhere green with straw.

And, flapping their wings, storks circle the town clock, stretch their necks straight into the wind and catch raindrops in their beaks.

And the burgomaster, who rarely gives anything much thought, rubs his double chin, and the lovelorn florist slowly wastes away, her gaze not wavering from one of her tulips.

And a minstrel swoons, buckling over her mandolin, and an old man plays a rommelpot, and some kid inflates a bladder, eager to begin his game.

And drinkers smoke in a murky dive, and a maid hangs a dead pheasant in a tavern window.

Moonlight
— translated by Gian Lombardo

Wake up sleepers,
And pray for your sins.
Town-crier's cry

Oh, how pleasant it is when the hour is struck in the steeple at night, how sweet to gaze at the moon, with her nose looking like a gold coin!

★

Two lepers wailed beneath my window. A dog howled at the crossroads. A cricket on my hearth chirped his prophecies very softly.

But before long my ear interrogated nothing more than a profound silence. The lepers returned to their huts to the sound of the jack-in-the-clock beating his wife.

The dog threaded its way down a small alley. It passed in front of the night watch's halberds that were covered with rust from the rain and chilled by the north wind.

The cricket fell asleep as soon as the last spark shed its final glimmer among the fireplace ashes.

And as for me, since fever breeds incoherency, it seemed that the moon's face was screwed up and her tongue dangled from her mouth like someone who had just been hung.

Gallows

— translated by Gian Lombardo

What do I see skulking about this gallows?

Faust.

Ah! What's that I'm hearing, perhaps evening's glancing kiss, or the hanged man heaving a sigh from the gibbet's crossbar?

Perhaps some cricket singing from its hiding-place in moss and amid barren ivy that dresses the wood out of pity?

Perhaps some fly in flight sounding its clarion to ears deaf to the hunter's tally-ho?

Perhaps some dung-beetle that plucks in its tottering flight a bloody hair from his bald skull?

Or perhaps some spider embroidering a muslin swatch as a neckerchief to choke his collar?

It's the angelus chiming across city walls, from beyond the horizon, and the hanged man's carcass the setting sun reddens.

Maurice de Guérin

The Centaur
— translated by Gian Lombardo

I was born in these mountain caves. The first moments of my life trickled into the shadows of my distant abode without disturbing the silence, just like this valley's river whose first drops fall from some weeping rock in a remote cavern. When our mothers near giving birth, they wander into those caverns, and in their furthest, most untamed recesses, in the dankest shadows, they drop, without issuing even a moan, fruit as taciturn as themselves. Their potent milk enables us to overcome whatever struggles such infants might have to endure without succumbing. Yet we leave our caves later than you leave your cradles. It's common knowledge among us that we need to withdraw from the world and safeguard our first stage of existence as days when we commune solely with the gods. My growth charted its own course almost entirely in the shadows where I had been born. The location of my abode was struck so deep into the mountain that I would never have known an exit existed if the winds, after turning and twisting so many times from that distant opening, had not sometimes cast me a sudden draught of freshness or storminess. Sometimes, too, my mother returned, swathed in scents from the valleys or drenched and dripping from the waters into which she often dove. However, when she returned, she never told me about those little valleys or their streams. Rather, I inhaled what emanated from her — which upset me — and I paced this way and that in the darkness. What, I asked myself, is this realm outside that has so much power over my mother? What reigns there that is so compelling that it so frequently beckons her? What's so unsettling out there that she comes home each time in such a differ-ent mood? Sometimes my mother would come back animated with a profound joy. Sometimes she'd be so sad, shuffling her feet or limping along. Even from a distance I could detect her good spirits in how she carried herself and directed her gaze. I felt her moods with every fiber of my being. But her anguish seized me most strongly and ensnared me much more deeply into conflicted brooding. In those moments, I worried about my own fortitude, recognizing that I possessed a force that could not be contained. It took hold of me, making me thrash my arms about or redouble my strides in the broad shadows of the cave. I started to realize — through the blows that I struck in the void and my frenzied steps I made there — what my arms must embrace and where my feet must bring me… Ever since I have wrapped my arms around the torsos of centaurs, the bodies of heroes and the trunks of oaks. My hands have touched rocks, waters, innumerable plants and cupped the most subtle impressions of the air. I lift them up during impenetrable and serene nights to intercept the breezes and then glean from them signs to guide my way. Look, Melampus, how worn my hooves are! And yet, as stiff as I am in the far reaches of old age, there are still days when, in broad daylight on mountain summits, waving my arms and summoning all the speed left in me, I bolt as I did in my youth — and for the same reasons.

These fits alternated with long absences without frantic movement. Since then, I no longer possessed any other feeling in my whole being than that of maturation, which little by little welled in me. Having lost my taste for those outbursts, and having withdrawn into an absolute peace, I tasted without adulteration the benevolence of the gods who surged within me. Calm and shadow governed my thirst for life's secret allure. Shadows who inhabit these mountain caverns, I owe to your silent care the mystic education that so tenaciously nourished me. Shadows, under your watch I have tasted life as pure as it can be — life as it emanated from the very heart of the gods! When I descended from your sanctuary into the light of day, I staggered and did not greet the light because it seized me so violently, drugging me as if it were a fatal potion suddenly coursing in my veins. I warrant that my being, until then so stable and uncomplicated, shuddered and lost much of itself as if leaves blown in the wind.

O Melampus, why do you want to learn about the lives of the centaurs? Which god's will guided you to me, the oldest and saddest of them all? It has been a long time since I practiced anything of their ways any more. I never leave this mountain top where old age has confined me. These days, I use my arrows only to uproot stubborn plants. Placid lakes still recognize me but rivers have forgotten me. Yet I will tell you some things about my youth. But, beware, those recollections issue from a corrupt memory and sputter like a stingy libation falling from a leaky urn. I have recounted my infancy without difficulty because it was tranquil and perfect. Life pure and simple filled me — it's easy to retain and recount those memories without sorrow. O Melampus, if a god were begged to retell his life, he would utter just a couple words!

So full of commotion, my youth passed quickly. I lived to move and my steps knew no bounds. Proud of my free-roaming, I wandered through every part of this wilderness. One day as I followed a gorge rarely visited by centaurs, I discovered a man who was skirting the river on the opposite bank. He was the first human that I had ever seen. I sneered at him. There, at most, I said to myself, goes only half of me! Look how minced his steps are and how cumbersome he carries himself! His eyes seem to measure space with sadness. Undoubtedly, he must be some centaur undone by the gods and reduced to scurrying like that.

In my forays I often spent much of my time refreshing myself by wading in river beds. Half of me would be hidden under water, struggling to keep upright so the other half would appear unruffled as I strode with my arms folded above the torrent. I lost myself thus among those waves, succumbing to their divagations that took me far and wide, which conveyed all the beauty of the riverbanks to their savage guest. How many times, surprised by nightfall, I floated along the current under lengthening shadows spreading the gods' nightly influence to the furthest reaches of the valleys! My impetuous life tempered then to the scantiest remnant of a single subtle feeling of existence diffused equally throughout my entire being, like the shimmering gleams of the goddess who traverses the nights in the waters where I swam. Melampus, my dotage makes me miss the rivers. The majority peaceful and monotonous, they accept their destinies more calmly than centaurs, and with a more constructive wisdom than men. When I left them, I was attended by their gifts that accompanied me day in and day out, and that dissipated only slowly, like all perfumes do.

A wild and blind inconstancy took hold of my steps. In the middle of the most furious dash, it sometimes occurred to me to break my stride suddenly, as if an abyss had opened up at my feet or a god blocked my path. These sudden stops fueled my fits even more. Sometimes I cut branches in the forests. I brandished them over my head as I ran. I ran so fast their leaves bent with barely a flutter but when I slowed and stopped, wind and movement returned to them, and they murmured and rustled again. Thus my life flickered in my very core except when I would suddenly erupt with one of my impetuous dashes through these valleys. I listened to my being's roiling flood, listened to it as it fed the flames that it had fanned in the expanse that I had just madly crossed. My quivering flanks struggled against the onrush that pressed inward on them, and tasted pleasure in the upheaval, known only to seashores, to corral without diminishment a fevered and excitable life. Meanwhile, with my head cocked to catch the wind's freshness, I observed how quickly the summits of the mountains had become so far away, as well as the tree-lined riverbanks and their waters — waters that followed a lazy course, and trees firmly rooted in the earth, with only their branches moving in the gusts of wind that made them groan. "I alone," I said to myself, "am free to move. I have lived my life from one end of these valleys to the other. I am happier than the torrents that cascade from the mountains never to return to their source. The sound of my steps is more beautiful than the creak of branches and rush of wave. That sound is the reverberation of a wandering centaur who has no guide but himself." So while my sweating flanks were drunk with my flight, I felt my pride surge and, turning my head, I paused for a while to behold my steaming croup.

Youth is like a verdant forest besieged by gales: it stirs up from every which way life's abundant gifts, always letting some haunting murmur reign in the foliage. Living amid the rivers' abandon, inhaling Cybele unceasingly, either in the river beds or on the peaks, I bounded everywhere living carefree and unfettered. When night, filled with a divine calm, found me on the slopes and led me to some caves' openings, it was there that I was pacified in the same way night stills the sea, letting abide in me those delicate undulations that forestall sleep without disturbing rest. Stretched out on the threshold of my retreat, my hindquarters hidden in the cave and my head under the sky, I watched the parade of shadows. Then those strange happenings that had so amazed me during the day escaped drop by drop, returning to Cybele's peaceful heart just as after a heavy rain the remaining drops clinging to the leaves fall and rejoin the waters below. It is said that during the night the sea gods abandon their palaces deep under the water's surface and, sitting upon headlands, they gaze upon the ocean's expanse. In like manner I kept watch, having at my feet a vast panorama of life similar to those gods' sleeping sea. Returned to a full and clear consciousness, I felt as if I had just been born, as if the core of the watery abyss that had conceived me left me high and dry on the top of the mountain, like Amphitrite's waves stranding a dolphin on the strand at low tide.

My gaze ranged widely and I espied even the most distant points. Like footprints on a sand bar, the western ridge of mountains retained impressions of sunset scintillations that darkness could not erase. Naked and pure summits persisted in pale clarity. I sometimes saw Pan descend there, always alone. Sometimes I also heard a choir of Orphic gods, or saw some mountain nymph pass by enraptured with night. Sometimes eagles from Mount Olympus flew to the heavens and vanished into distant constellations or roosted in sacred groves. The spirit of the gods, bestirring themselves, suddenly shattered the ancient oaks' tranquility.

Melampus, you seek wisdom, which is the science of the gods' will. You wander among your kind, a mortal waylaid by destiny. In this land, there's a stone that, when touched, issues a sound similar to that of an instrument's string breaking. It has been said that Apollo, who tended his sheep in this wilderness, placed his lyre on that stone, abandoning its melody there. O Melampus, wandering gods set their lyres on stones but no one… none forgot one there. During the time when I kept watch in the caves, I sometimes believed that I was going to surprise the dreams of a sleeping Cybele, and that the mother of gods, betrayed by her dreams, would part with some of her secrets in her sleep. Yet I never discovered any sound save what dissolved in night's whispers or dissolved in the indistinct words from raging rivers.

"O Macareus," one day great Chiron, whom I cared for in his old age, said to me, "we are both centaurs of the mountains but our temperaments are so different! You see, I directed all of my attention to the study of plants. You, on the other hand, you are like those mortals who collect water or firewood or bring to their lips some pieces of Pan's broken reedpipe. Consequently, those mortals, having inhaled what remains of a god's breath from those pipes, become possessed by a wild spirit or perhaps erupt in some strange frenzy. Restless and seized by an unknown purpose, they set out into the wilderness, plunge themselves into the forests, skirt waterways, become one with the mountains. Mares beloved by winds in distant Scythia are neither wilder than you nor sadder in the evening after the North Wind has died down. Do you want to know the gods, Macareus? Do you want to know from whence men, animals and the principles of universal fire come? Ancient Ocean, father of all, keeps these things secret to himself. His attendant nymphs describe a choir circling around him and constantly sing to drown out anything that might escape from his lips during sleep. Mortals who touched the gods because they were virtuous received lyres from them to delight whomever might hear them, or novel seeds that enrich them — but nothing from the gods' unyielding mouths.

"In my youth, Apollo disposed me towards plants, and taught me how to extract beneficial sap from their veins. Since then, I have steadfastly confined myself to the great abode of these mountains, unsettled, unceasingly occupying myself in the search for simples, and in communicating the healing properties that I discover. Do you see from here the bald peak of Mount Oeta? Alcide laid it bare to build his funeral pyre. O Macareus! the demigod children of the gods heap lion skins on their pyres and are consumed on desolate mountaintops! The poisons of the earth taint blood derived from the immortal ones! And we centaurs, begotten by a reckless mortal paired with a goddess clothed as a cloud, what aid could we ever hope for from Jupiter who struck down the father of our race? The gods' vulture eternally rends the entrails of the artisan who shaped the first man. O Macareus! men and centaurs acknowledge as authors of their blood those who stole the privilege from the immortals. Perhaps whatever is beyond them is only what has been robbed from them, what is only the slightest mote of their nature dispersed far and wide, as if it were a flitting seed borne on the all-powerful wind of destiny. It is well known that Aegeus, father of Theseus, hid keepsakes and proofs under a rock by the sea with which his son could one day recognize his birth. The jealous gods have hidden somewhere testimony of the origin of everything, but at the edge of what ocean did they roll the stone that covers that evidence, O Macareus!"

Such was the wisdom great Chiron conveyed to me. Reduced to the last reaches of old age, that centaur nourished the noblest discourse in his spirit. His still robust body scarcely deviated from the straight by only the slightest pitch, as if he were an oak tree beset by wind. The force of his steps hardly suffered from age's debits. It could be said that he retained vestiges of the immortality he once received from Apollo but that had since been rendered back to that god.

As for myself, Melampus, I wither into decrepitude, tranquil as the setting constellations. Yet I still retain enough headstrongness to clamber onto rocks where I'll then loiter, either to survey the wild and restless clouds, or to watch the weepy Hyades, the Pleiades or bright Orion rise from the horizon. I know that I am fading, quickly melting away like a snowflake landing on water. Soon I will mingle with the rivers that flow into the deepest reaches of the earth.

Ivan Turgenev

The Insect
— *translated by Marianna Rosen*

I dreamed that about twenty of us were sitting in a large room with open windows.

Among us were women, children, old men....We were all talking about something quite ordinary, talking chaotically.

Suddenly, with a sharp crackle there flew into the room a large insect, about four inches long... it flew in, circled around, and settled on a wall.

It resembled a fly or a wasp. Its trunk was the color of dirt, same too with the color of its flat stiff wings; splayed hairy legs and a head, angular and thick, like a darner's; and this head and legs were bright-red, as if soaked in blood.

This strange insect was incessantly turning its head, up and down, to the right and to the left, shifting its legs...then it suddenly darted off the wall and flew with a rustling sound about the room—then, having settled again on a wall, it horridly and loathsomely squirmed, without leaving its spot.

In all of us it evoked revulsion, fear, even horror....None of us had ever seen anything like that, everyone screamed, "Get this monster out of here!", swaying their handkerchiefs from a distance...for no one dared to approach it...and when the insect took off — everyone recoiled.

Only one of our companions, still young, pale, stared at us all with bemusement. He shrugged his shoulders, he smiled — he positively could not understand what was the matter with us and why we were so agitated? He did not see the insect — did not hear the sinister crackle of its wings.

All of a sudden, the insect seemed to fix its gaze on him, shot up, landed on his head, and stung him on the forehead above the eyes… the youth gasped faintly—and fell dead.

The terrible fly flew out at once…. Only then did we realize what our guest was.

The Skulls

— translated by Marianna Rosen

An opulent, extravagantly lit hall; a large group of ladies and gentlemen.

Faces enlivened, excited speech... A raucous conversation is carrying on about a famous singer. She is called divine, immortal... Oh, how nicely yesterday she warbled her final trill!

And suddenly — as if by the wave of a magic wand — from all the heads and all the faces a thin husk of skin began to peel, exposing suddenly the skulls' deathly pallor; and the bluish tin of their bones and gums began to flicker.

I watched with horror how those gums and bones shuddered and shook; how, glistening in the light of lamps and candles, those bony gnarled orbs twisted, and how those eyeballs rolled in them, these other senseless orbs.

I didn't dare to touch my own face, I didn't dare to look at myself in the mirror.

And the skulls twisted as before...And with the same old raucous, red rags that fluttered through bared teeth, those wagging tongues, still babbled how wonderfully and inimitably the immortal, yes, immortal singer warbled her final trill!

Charles Baudelaire

Everyman his Chimæra
— *translated by James Huneker*

Beneath a broad grey sky, upon a vast and dusty plain devoid of grass, and where not even a nettle or a thistle was to be seen, I met several men who walked bowed down to the ground.

Each one carried upon his back an enormous Chimæra as heavy as a sack of flour or coal, or as the equipment of a Roman foot-soldier.

But the monstrous beast was not a dead weight, rather she enveloped and oppressed the men with her powerful and elastic muscles, and clawed with her two vast talons at the breast of her mount. Her fabulous head reposed upon the brow of the man like one of those horrible casques by which ancient warriors hoped to add to the terrors of the enemy.

I questioned one of the men, asking him why they went so. He replied that he knew nothing, neither he nor the others, but that evidently they went somewhere, since they were urged on by an unconquerable desire to walk.

Very curiously, none of the wayfarers seemed to be irritated by the ferocious beast hanging at his neck and cleaving to his back: one had said that he considered it as a part of himself. These grave and weary faces bore witness to no despair. Beneath the splenetic cupola of the heavens, their feet trudging through the dust of an earth as desolate as the sky, they journeyed onwards with the resigned faces of men condemned to hope for ever. So the train passed me and faded into the atmosphere of the horizon at the place where the planet unveils herself to the curiosity of the human eye.

During several moments I obstinately endeavoured to comprehend this mystery; but irresistible Indifference soon threw herself upon me, nor was I more heavily dejected thereby than they by their crushing Chimæras.

The Invitation to the Voyage

— translated by James Huneker

It is a superb land, a country of Cockaigne, as they say, that I dream of visiting with an old friend. A strange land, drowned in our northern fogs, that one might call the East of the West, the China of Europe; a land patiently and luxuriously decorated with the wise, delicate vegetations of a warm and capricious phantasy.

A true land of Cockaigne, where all is beautiful, rich, tranquil, and honest; where luxury is pleased to mirror itself in order; where life is opulent, and sweet to breathe; from whence disorder, turbulence, and the unforeseen are excluded; where happiness is married to silence; where even the food is poetic, rich and exciting at the same time; where all things, my beloved, are like you.

Do you know that feverish malady that seizes hold of us in our cold miseries; that nostalgia of a land unknown; that anguish of curiosity? It is a land which resembles you, where all is beautiful, rich, tranquil and honest, where phantasy has built and decorated an occidental China, where life is sweet to breathe, and happiness married to silence. It is there that one would live; there that one would die.

Yes, it is there that one must go to breathe, to dream, and to lengthen one's hours by an infinity of sensations. A musician has written the "Invitation to the Waltz"; where is he who will write the "Invitation to the Voyage," that one may offer it to his beloved, to the sister of his election?

Yes, it is in this atmosphere that it would be good to live,—yonder, where slower hours contain more thoughts, where the clocks strike the hours of happiness with a more profound and significant solemnity.

Upon the shining panels, or upon skins gilded with a sombre opulence, beatified paintings have a discreet life, as calm and profound as the souls of the artists who created them.

The setting suns that colour the rooms and salons with so rich a light, shine through veils of rich tapestry, or through high leaden-worked windows of many compartments. The furniture is massive, curious, and bizarre, armed with locks and secrets, like profound and refined souls. The mirrors, the metals, the ail ver work and the china, play a mute and mysterious symphony for the eyes; and from all things, from the corners, from the chinks in the drawers, from the folds of drapery, a singular perfume escapes, a Sumatran *revenez-y,* which is like the soul of the apartment.

A true country of Cockaigne, I have said; where all is rich, correct and shining, like a beautiful conscience, or a splendid set of silver, or a medley of jewels. The treasures of the world flow there, as in the house of a laborious man who has well merited the entire world. A singular land, as superior to others as Art is superior to Nature; where Nature is made over again by dream; where she is corrected, embellished, refashioned.

Let them seek and seek again, let them extend the limits of their happiness for ever, these alchemists who work with flowers! Let them offer a prize of sixty or a hundred thousand florins to whosoever can solve their ambitious problems! As for me, I have found my *black tulip* and my *blue dahlia!*

Incomparable flower, tulip found at last, symboli-cal dahlia, it is there, is it not, in this so calm and dreamy land that you live and blossom? Will you not there be framed in your proper analogy, and will you not be mirrored, to speak like the mystics, in your own *correspondence?*

Dreams!—always dreams! and the more ambitious and delicate the soul, the farther from possibility is the dream. Every man carries within him his dose of natural opium, incessantly secreted and renewed, and, from birth to death, how many hours can we count that have been filled with positive joy, with successful and decided action? Shall we ever live in and become a part of the picture my spirit has painted, the picture that resembles you?

These treasures, furnishings, luxury, order, perfumes and miraculous flowers, are you. You again are the great rivers and calm canals. The enormous ships drifting beneath their loads of riches, and musical with the sailors' monotonous song, are my thoughts that sleep and stir upon your breast. You take them gently to the sea that is Infinity, reflecting the profundities of the sky in the limpid waters of your lovely soul;—and when, outworn by the surge and gorged with the products of the Orient, the ships come back to the ports of home, they are still my thoughts, grown rich, that have returned to you from Infinity.

Mademoiselle Bistoury
— *translated by Richard Sieburth*

As I was reaching the outskirts of town, beneath the glow of the gas lamps, I felt an arm softly slip around mine, and heard a voice at my ear: "Sir, are you a doctor?"

I looked up: she was a tall, well-built girl, wide-eyed, slightly rouged, her hair and bonnet strings fluttering in the wind.

"No; I am not a doctor. Let me pass."

"Of course you are! I can tell you're a doctor. Come to my place. I'll show you a good time. Come on!"

"I'll be sure to pay you a visit, but later, after the doctor's, damn it…"

"Aha!," she said, still clinging to my arm and bursting into laughter, "You're a doctor with a sense of humor, I've known several of your kind. Come on!"

I'm a passionate devotee of mystery, because I always set such high hopes on untangling it. So I allowed myself to be escorted away by this companion, or rather, by this unexpected enigma.

I'll skip the description of her hovel; you can find it in any number of well-known French poets of old. Except that (a detail Régnier missed) two or three portraits of famous doctors hung on the walls.

How she pampered me! Blazing fire, mulled wine, cigars; and as she was plying me with all these fine things, this ludicrous creature said to me, as she lit herself a cigar: "Make yourself at home, my friend, feel completely at your ease. It'll remind you of your younger days at the hospital. My Lord! Where did you come by all these white hairs? This is not the way you looked, not that long ago either, when you were interning with L… I remember your acting as his assistant on major operations. Now there was a man who really liked to slice and dice it up. And you were the fellow who'd used to hand him his instruments, his thread, his sponges. And once the operation was complete, he'd check his watch and proudly announce: 'Five minutes, gentlemen!' Oh yes, I do get around. I know all these gentlemen quite well."

A few minutes later, now addressing me in more familiar fashion, she again returned to the same old tune: "You're a doctor, aren't you, sweetheart?"

This senseless refrain brought me to me feet: "No I'm not," I shouted in anger.

"A surgeon, perhaps?"

"No! and no again!—unless I got it into my mind to cut off your head! God damn your blasted eyes!"

"Wait," she went on, "you'll see."

And she pulled out a stack of sheets from an armoire—it turned out to be a portfolio of portraits of illustrious doctors of the day, that collection of lithographs by Maurin★ which had been on display for a number of years on the quai Voltaire.

"Here! You recognize this one?"

"Yes. It's X. His name is there at the bottom of the picture; I happen to know him personally."

"See, I told you so! Here! That's Z., who used to say of X. in his lectures: 'This monster wears the blackness of his soul on his very face.' All because X. had had a professional disagreement with him. Everybody got such a laugh out of this back in Medical School. You remember? Here! That's K., who turned the revolutionaries he was treating at his hospital over to the government—that was back during the riots. How could a man that handsome be so heartless? That's W., a famous British doctor; I scooped him up during his visit to Paris. He looks like a fine young lady, doesn't he?"

I was fingering a string-wrapped packet lying nearby on the pedestal table. "Hold off a minute," she said, "those are the residents; and this packet here is the non-residents."

And she arrayed the bunch of photographic images into a fan; the faces pictured on them were indeed far younger.

"The next time we meet, you'll give me a picture of yourself, won't you, honey?"

"But," I said, returning to the question that was preying on my mind, "Why do you insist on taking me for doctor?"

"Because you are such a gentleman and so nice to the ladies."

"What twisted logic," I thought to myself.

"Mind me, I never make a mistake; I have known a great number of them. I have such a liking for these gentleman that even if there's nothing medically wrong with me, I occasionally make appointments with them, just to drop by. There are those who react quite coldly: "But there is nothing wrong with you whatsoever." But there are others who are more understanding, because I flirt around with them."

"And what if they don't understand…?"

"Well, in that case, since I have inconvenienced them for no good reason, I just leave them ten francs on the mantelpiece. They're so nice and sweet, these fellows! At the Pitié Hospital, I discovered a young intern—as pretty as an angel, and so polite, so hard-working, the poor boy! His fellow students told me that he was penniless because his parents were too poor to put him through school. This gave me confidence. After all, I'm a fairly good-looking woman, even if I'm getting a little on in years. I said to him: 'Come see me, come as often as you want. With me, no need to feel embarrassed. I don't need the money.' But, mind you, I didn't put it to him that crudely, I just hinted around: I was so afraid of humiliating him, sweet thing that he was. You may find this hard to believe, but I have this little quirk that I can't bring myself to admit to him. I'd like him to come see me with his doctor's kit and apron—perhaps with a few bloodstains on it!"

She said this quite straightforwardly, the way a sensitive man might ask the actress he was in love with: "I'd like to see you in that costume you wore for your first starring role."

Ever persistent, I continued on: "Can you remember the time or occasion when you first experienced this rather peculiar urge?"

I had difficulty making myself understood; at long last, I managed to get through. But she seemed quite crestfallen and, if I remember correctly, averted her eyes: "I have no idea… I can't remember."

What bizarre things one comes across in a large city, if one walks around with one's eyes open. Life teems with innocent monsters.

O Lord, my God—you the Creator, the Almighty; you who have granted us both Liberty and Law; you, the sovereign who allows men do as they will; you, the judge who pardons; you who have so many hidden ways, and who has perhaps instilled this taste for horror in my mind to convert my heart—like a cure at the tip of a scalpel. Lord, have pity on madmen and madwomen! O Creator, can monsters truly exist in the eyes of the One who alone knows why they exist, how they came to be what they are, and how they might not have become what they are?

Let's Beat Up the Poor!
— *translated by Richard Sieburth*

I had confined myself to my room for a fortnight, holed up with the sorts of books that were all the rage back then (sixteen or seventeen years ago)—i.e. books dealing with the art of making the masses healthy, wealthy and wise in twenty-four hours. I had therefore digested—or should I say, wolfed down—all the pedantic fare of these purveyors of public happiness, some exhorting the poor to become slaves, others persuading them that every pauper is a dethroned king. No surprise, then, if I found myself in a state of mind verging on vertigo—or idiocy.

Yet I somehow seemed to sense, stirring in the depths of my intellect, the inkling of an idea far superior to the entire catalogue of old wives' remedies that I had just been perusing. But it was no more than the idea of an idea, something as of yet infinitely vague.

So I ventured outdoors, dying of thirst—for the severe addiction to trashy books creates a proportional craving for fresh air and cool drinks.

As I was about to enter a pub, a beggar held out his hat to me, shooting me one of those unforgettable looks that could topple thrones—if mind could move matter, or the eye of a mesmerist ripen grapes.

At that very moment, I heard a voice whispering into my ear, one I immediately recognized; it was the voice of that good Angel—or good Demon—who is always by my side. If Socrates had his good Demon, why shouldn't I have my good Angel?

Why shouldn't I be honored as Socrates has been of late—issued a certificate of insanity signed by the artful Dr. Lélut and the knowledgeable Dr. Baillarger?

The Demon of Socrates differs from mine in that the former would only manifest itself to the philosopher in order forbid, warn, hinder him, whereas mine favors me with counsel, suggestion, persuasion. Poor old Socrates had a Demon who was merely prohibitive; mine works in the affirmative. Mine's a Demon of action—a fighter Demon.

So this is what its voice was whispering to me: "To truly be some-one else's equal, you have to prove it; to truly be worthy of liberty, you have to conquer it."

I immediately lunged out at my beggar. With a single punch, I blackened his eye, which within the space of second swelled up like ball. I broke one of my nails as I relieved him of two of his teeth; and since I didn't feel I had the strength to deliver the knock-out blow to the old fellow (being of delicate disposition and having rarely boxed), I grabbed his collar with one hand while I caught his throat with the other, and then proceeded to vigorously bash his head against the wall. I must admit that I had previously inspected the neighborhood with a quick glance, making sure that no policeman would disturb me in this deserted suburb any time soon.

Having finally knocked the weakened sexagenarian to the ground with a kick in the back energetic enough to break his shoulder-blades, I grabbed a thick tree branch that was lying nearby and pounded him with the obstinate energy of a cook trying to tenderize a piece of steak.

Suddenly—O what a miracle! O what a joy for the philosopher verifying the excellence of his theory!—I saw the ancient carcass turn over and rise to its feet with an energy I would have never suspected in a machine so utterly thrown out of whack. With a look of hate that struck me as quite *auspicious,* the decrepit desperado flailed out at me, blackening my two eyes, breaking four of my teeth, and, taking up the same tree branch, beat the living daylights out of me. The energetic medication that I had administered to him had restored his pride and his life.

I finally managed to signal to him that I now considered the dis-cussion closed, and getting back up on my feet, as satisfied as a Sophist of old, I said to him: "Sir, *you are my equal!* Please do me the honor of sharing my purse with you; and, should any of your colleagues ask you for a handout, don't forget (if you are truly a philanthropist) to apply the theory that it has been my *pain* to test out on your back."

He heartily swore that he had understood my theory and that he would obey my advice.

"What do you have to say to this, Citizen Proudhon?"

Stéphane Mallarmé

Reminiscence
— translated by Rosemary Lloyd

Orphaned, I wandered clothed in black and my eyes devoid of family:
in the square, holiday tents unfolded. Did I sense the future and know
that I would be like them? I loved the smell of the wanderers, went to
them to forget my comrades. No chorus decrying the separation, no
far-off harangue, the drama demanding the holy hour of the lamp, I
sought to speak with a child too unsteady to appear with his race,
wearing a night cap cut like Dante's hood. He was already sucking
into himself, in the form of a soft cheese sandwich, the snows of
mountain tops, the lily, or another whiteness constituting inner wings:
I would have begged him to admit me to his superior meal, shared
swiftly with some famous donkey which had leapt forth against a
nearby canvas in the course of the highlights and banalities linked to
the day. Naked, pirouetting in the nimbleness of his leotard, astonish-
ing to me, he, who moreover was the one to begin: "And your par-
ents?" "I have none". "Come, if you knew how funny a father is…just
the other week when the soup was slow to boil, he was making faces
as good as when the boss hands out slaps and kicks. My friend!" And
he triumphantly raised his leg to me with glorious ease: "he amazes
us, my dad," then he bit into the chaste feast of the very young: "Your
mom, perhaps you don't have one, since you're alone? Mine eats tow
and everyone claps their hands. No kidding, parents are funny people,
who make you laugh." The parade exalted and he left: As for me, I
sighed, suddenly saddened at my lack of family.

The Priest

— translated by Rosemary Lloyd

Spring pushes the organism to acts that, in another season, are unknown to it and many a historical treatise abounds in descriptions of this phenomenon in animals. How much more plausibly interesting it would be to gather some of the changes that the seasonal moment brings to the behavior of individuals formed for a spiritual life! With the irony of winter still clinging to me, I for my part remember a state that remains equivocal, provided I do not substitute an absolute or naïve naturalism, but remain capable of pursuing a sense of pleasure in differentiating between certain sprigs of herbs. Since nothing in the case before us brings any profit to the crowd, I escaped, to cogitate on it, under some shady places surrounding yesterday's town. So, it is from their almost banal mystery that I will put on show an accessible and striking example of spring inspirations.

Just recently, in a little-frequented spot in the Bois de Bolougne, I was sharply surprised when, as a dark low agitation, I saw, through the thousand interstices of shrubs good for hiding nothing, complete and from the beating of the three-cornered hat right to the tips of shoes strengthened by silver buckles, a priest, who, far from witnesses, was responding to the solicitations of the grass. The only thing that pleased me (and nothing similar serves divine schemes) was that, as guilty as someone pretending to be scandalized and seizing a pebble from the path, I gathered up through my smile, even one of understanding, a blush on the face, veiled by both hands, of this poor man, a blush other than that no doubt caused by his solitary exercise! Swift of foot, I was forced, in order not to distract him by my presence, to draw on my skill; and strong against the temptation of looking back, I imagined the almost diabolical apparition that went on crumpling the renewal of his ribs, right, left, and on the stomach, obtaining a chaste frenzy. Every-thing, rubbing or stretching the limbs, rolling, sliding, led to satisfac-tion: and stopping, forbidden to the tickling of some high spear of flowers on black calves, amid that special dress worn with the appear-ance that you are, for yourself, at least your own wife. Solitude, the cold silence spread through the verdure, perceived by senses not so much subtle as anxious, you experienced the furious clatter of a fabric; as if the abstruse night of its folds were at last shaken out! and the muffled shocks of the rejuvenated skeleton against the earth; but the eccentric had no need to contemplate you. Hilarious, it was enough to search in oneself the cause of a pleasure or a duty, insufficiently explained by a return, on seeing a lawn, of a seminarian's frolicking. The influence of spring's breath gently dilating the immutable texts written on the flesh, he too, emboldened by a disturbance that pleased his sterile thought, had come to recognize through a contact with Nature, immediate, marked, violent, positive, stripped of all intellectual curiosity, a general well-being; and candidly, far from the obedience and constraint of his occupation, from the canons, interdictions, censures, he rolled, in the beatitude of his innate simplicity, happier than a donkey. That the aim of his completed promenade should have been, immediately and completely, heightened, not without shaking off the pistils and wiping off the sap attached to his person, and the hero of my vision returned unnoticed to the crowd and to the habits of his ministry, I wouldn't dream of denying any of that; but I have the right not to take it into account. Isn't my discretion regarding the frolics I at first glimpsed recompensed by fixing them forever like the reverie of a passer-by pleased with contemplating it, an image stamped with the mysterious seal of modernity, simultaneously baroque and beautiful?

Glory
— translated by Rosemary Lloyd

Glory! I only discovered it yesterday, incontrovertible, and nothing that someone else calls by that name can interest me.

Traitors to the word, a hundred posters espousing the days' misunderstood gold have fled, as if to all corners of the town, my eyes drawn low to the horizon by a departure of the rail before a meditation on the obscure pride granted by an approach of the forest in the season of its apotheosis.

Sole discord amid the exaltation of the hour, a shout traduced that name, known for displaying the continuity of slowly disappearing summits, Fontainebleau, that I meditated, the window of the compartment assaulted, a fist also strangling the interrupting throat: Silence! Let no indifferent yap reveal the shadows that here have insinuated themselves into my mind as the carriage doors flap under an inspired egalitarian wind, as the omnipresent tourists are vomited out. A mendacious silence of rich woods suspends around us some extraordinary state of illusion, what do you reply to me? that they, these travelers, have departed today for your station, leaving the capital, that good employer whose duty is to bellow and from which I expect, far from seizing an intoxication allotted to all by the combined liberalities of nature and the State, nothing but a stillness extended long enough to allow me to isolate myself from the urban delegation in the ecstatic torpor of the leaves over there, leaves too immobilized for a crisis not to scatter them soon in the air; here, without affronting your integrity, take this coin.

An inattentive uniform inviting me to some barrier or other, I hand over without a word, in place of a metal seduction, my ticket.

Obeyed nevertheless, yes, to see nothing but the asphalt spreading free of footprints, for I cannot yet imagine, in the pomp of this exceptional October while the thousand existences display their vacuity as an enormous monotony of capital whose haunting will disappear from here when the whistle blows in the fog, that any furtive escapee except me has felt that this year there is, bitter and luminous sobs, many an indecisive floating of ideas deserting perils as they desert branches, a certain shudder, and what makes one think of autumn under the skies.

No one and, the arms of doubt blown away like those who also carry their share of a secret splendor, too appreciable a trophy to appear! but, not without suddenly hurling myself into that diurnal gaze of immortal trunks watching over the unloading of one of the super-human sources of pride (well, isn't it necessary to recognize its authenticity?) or passing the threshold where, in a high guard, torches burn away everything dreamt before their outburst as their crimson broadcasts in the cloud the universal consecration of the royal intruder who had only to come: I waited, to be that intruder, for the slow return to ordinary movement to reduce to its proportions of a childish chimera carrying the crowd away somewhere, the train that had deposited me there alone.

Judith Gautier

The Fisherman
— *translated by Stuart Merrill*

[after Li-Taï-Pé]

The earth has drunk the snow, and now are seen once more the blossoms of the plum-tree.

The leaves of the willow are like new gold, and the lake seems a lake of silver.

Now is the time when the butterflies powdered with sulphur rest their velvety heads upon the hearts of the flowers.

The fisherman, from his motionless boat, casts forth his nets, breaking the surface of the water.

He thinks of her who stays at home like the swallow in her nest, of her whom he will soon see again, when he brings her food, like the swallow's mate.

By the River
— translated by Stuart Merrill

[after Li-Taï-Pé]

The young girls have gone down to the river; they sink among the tufts of lilies.

They cannot be seen, but their laughter is heard, and the wind blows perfumes from their dresses.

A young man on horseback passes by the edge of the river, close to the young girls.

One of them has felt her heart beat, and her face has changed color.

But the tufts of lilies close around him.

Joris-Karl Huysmans

Camaïeu in Red
— translated by Stuart Merrill

The room was hung with pink satin embossed with crimson sprays; the curtains fell amply from the windows, breaking their great folds of garnet velvet upon a purple-flowered carpet. On the walls were suspended sanguines by Boucher, and platters of brass gemmed and inlaid with niello by some artist of the Renaissance.

The divan, the arm-chairs, the chairs, were covered with stuffs similar to the hangings, with carnation fringes; and upon the mantle, surmounted by a glass that revealed an autumnal sky all empurpled by the setting sun and forests with leaves as red as wine, bloomed, in a vast stand, an enormous bouquet of carmine azaleas, of sage, of digitalis, and of amaranth.

The all-powerful goddess was buried in the cushions of the divan, rubbing her tawny tresses against the cherry-red satin, displaying her pink skirts, twirling her little morocco slipper at the end of her foot. She sighed affectedly, arose, stretched her arms, seized a large-bellied bottle, and poured out in a small glass, with slender stem and wrought in the shape of a vise, a thread of reddishbrown port.

At that moment the sun inundated the boudoir with its red gleams, struck scintillating flashes from the spirals of the glass, caused the ambrosial liquor to sparkle like molten topazes, and, shattering its rays against the brass of the platters, lighted in it fulgurating fires. It was a rutilant confusion of flames against which stood out the features of the drinker, like those of the virgins of Cimabue and Angelico, whose heads are encircled with a nimbus of gold.

That fanfare of red stunned me; that gamut of furious intensity, of impossible violence, blinded me. I closed my eyes, and when I opened them once more, the dazzling tint had vanished, the sun had set! Since that time the red boudoir and the drinker have disappeared; the magic blaze is extinguished.

In summer, however, when the nostalgia of red weighs more heavily upon me, I raise my head to the sun, and there, under its hot stings, impassible, with eyes obstinately closed, I see under the veil of my lids a red vapor; I recall my thoughts, and I see once more, for a minute, for a second, the disquieting fascination, the unforgotten enchantment.

Arthur Rimbaud

City
— *translated by Mark Polizzotti*

I am the transitory and not too disgruntled citizen of a metropolis considered modern because any appreciable taste has been evaded, in the furnishings and facades of houses as in the city plan. You'll find no trace here of any monument to superstition. Morals and language have been reduced to their simplest expression, at last! These millions of people, who don't need to know each other, conduct their education, trade, and old age so uniformly that their lifespans must be many times shorter than the insane statistics for continental populations. And so as I watch from my window new specters, new Furies, gliding through the dense, eternal soot — our sylvan shadow, our summer night! — past my cottage which is my country and all my heart, since everything here looks the same: Death without tears, our active maidservant; and a desperate Cupid; and a handsome Crime whimpering in the street filth.

Mystic
— translated by Mark Polizzotti

On the embankment slope, angels twirl their woolen robes in pastures of emerald and steel.

Fields of flame leap to the crest of the knoll. To the left, the fertile ground of the ridge is trampled by hordes of murder and war, and all the sounds of disaster curve off in their wake. Behind the right-hand ridge is the eastern line, the line of progress.

And while the swirling, leaping roar of conch shells and human nights forms the upper part of the scene,

The gentle flowering of the stars and sky and everything else descends toward the embankment, like a basket, against our face, and fashions the blue floral abyss down below.

from *Alchemy of the Word*
   — *translated by Mark Polizzotti*

My turn. The tale of one of my follies.

For so long I boasted ownership of every possible landscape, sneered at the sacred cows of painting and modern poetry.

I loved inane paintings, lintel decorations, stage sets, acrobats' backdrops, shop signs, garish prints; outmoded literature, church Latin, pornographic booklets riddled with typos, the novels of our forebears, fairy tales, small children's books, old operas, corny refrains, naïve rhythms.

I dreamed of crusades, voyages of discovery that left no trace, republics with no history, suppressed religious wars, revolutions in mores, great drifts of races and continents; I believed unconditionally in magic.

I invented the color of vowels! — *A* black, *E* white, *I* red, *O* blue, *U* green — regulated the shape and movement of each consonant. With intuitive rhythms I prided myself on inventing the poetic Word that *all the senses* could access, someday. I reserved translation rights.

At first it was a study. I transcribed silences and nights, recorded the inexpressible. I captured frenzies.

Oscar Wilde

The Artist

One evening there came into his soul the desire to fashion an image of *The Pleasure that Abideth for a Moment*. And he went forth into the world to look for bronze. For he could think only in bronze.

But all the bronze of the whole world had disappeared, nor anywhere in the whole world was there any bronze to be found, save only the bronze of the image of *The Sorrow that Endureth For Ever*.

Now this image he had himself, and with his own hands, fashioned, and had set it on the tomb of the one thing he had loved in life. On the tomb of the dead thing he had most loved had he set this image of his own fashioning, that it might serve as a sign of the love of man that dieth not, and a symbol of the sorrow of man that endureth for ever. And in the whole world there was no other bronze save the bronze of this image.

And he took the image he had fashioned, and set it in a great furnace, and gave it to the fire.

And out of the bronze of the image of *The Sorrow that Endureth For Ever* he fashioned an image of *The Pleasure that Abideth for a Moment*.

Fiona Macleod (William Sharp)

The White Merle

Long, long ago, a white merle flew out of Eden. Its song has been in the world ever since, but few there are who have seen the flash of its white wings through the green gloom of the living wood—the sun-splashed, rain-drenched, mist-girt, storm-beat wood of human life.

But to-day, as I came through the wood, under an arch of tempest, and led by lightnings, I passed into a green sun-splashed place.

There, there, I heard the singing of a rapt song of joy ! there, ah, there I saw the flash of white wings !

Frans Erens

Golden Song
— *translated by John Irons*

A golden expanse, the heath lies wide.

The brook roots through the sandy soil: it slithers along in twists and
turns.

In the light of the evening sun and one by one the golden plovers
rise. They hang up high in the light-blue sky. They call to each other
with golden weeps of woe.

On their wide-spread wings they hang in the pale-blue shivering sky
and on the banks of the brook they let their gold-murmurings roll in
drawn-out strings of rounded gentle sound.

Like the golden music of golden heath a-quiver with heat there falls
from above from pure-crystal rarefied air the trailing gold trilling of
drifting golden plovers and upwards from the ground, towards the
distant horizon the gold-organing song-calls drift in the silence. Then
it is silent once more and once more the golden monotonous trilling
resumes.

Then the even surface of sound hovers transparently pure in the lofty
air. Then the rippling monotonous sound rolls on with a falling, final
weep.

They call out of earth-woe, their woes loud with gurgling golden
tones; the soul-fall of sheer loneliness and cheerful woe-weeping,
jubilant joy, the lament of lonesomeness, the vanity of vanities.

Masaoka Shiki

A Dog
— *translated by Scott Mehl*

It's a long story, but I'll be brief. In India long ago there was the king-
dom of Guddha-Dhoghi, ruled by King Bau-vau. This king and all his
people were exceedingly fond of dogs.

Imagine the furor, then, when one of the king's subjects killed the
king's favorite dog.

Not only was the man put to death for his transgression; he was re-
born as a dog in Shinano, the coldest region in Japan, the most remote
and insignificant country in the world.

Now, Shinano is mountainous, and there are no fish to be had, so the
dog went to Ubasuteyama, surviving by eating the old women who
had been abandoned there to die. Such was the wretchedness of his
new existence.

One evening, when he had just eaten his eighty-eighth old woman,
he saw the first star in the night sky. On seeing its light, he had a
sudden realization: being a dog as he was, it was a terrible sin to eat
human beings. He immediately made his way to the Zenkōji Temple
and confessed all his sins, praying to be reborn as a man. For seven
days and seven nights he prayed continuously, passing the nighttime
hours under the temple veranda.

On the eighth night, a little Buddha Amitābha came to the dog's bed-
side and augustly said, "In recognition of your meritorious devotion,
your prayers will be answered. May your heart remain full of faith and
may you never waver. The aspiration for Buddhahood may become
manifest even in a beast such as yourself."[5]

Awaking from this dream, the dog felt buoyed by the deity's words. He resolved to go on a pilgrimage, traveling from province to province and stopping at sacred sites, where he would perform rites of mourning for the women he had eaten. So doing, he would bring about the fulfillment of his wish to be reborn a man.

And so he went, proceeding from cemetery to cemetery. Finally he made the crossing to the island of Shikoku, where there are eighty-eight holy sites on a pilgrimage route. At the first of these he sought absolution for the killing of the first woman, at the second the second, and so on. Howling prayers to the spirit of Kōbō-Daishi[6] all along his route, he made haste.

When he had thus performed obsequies at eighty-seven of the holy sites on Shikoku and arrived at last at the temple gate at the eighty-eighth, he collapsed in a faint. Whining piteously, he raised his head, and saw standing before him a jizō.[7] The jizō had no nose. To the jizō the dog said, "I beg you humbly to erect a signpost at the crossroads of the six paths of rebirth, pointing the way toward the human world. If you grant my prayer, then when I'm reborn, I will give you a bib made of fine red muslin."

"I accept your offer, and I will make your prayer come true," the jizō said.

Hearing this, the dog was so happy that he ran in a circle three times, yipping delightedly, and died. Soon, out of nowhere crows gathered, eighty-eight of them in all. The crows—terrifying to behold!—descended upon the dog's corpse and commenced feasting upon the body from head to tail.

An itinerant priest who was passing by saw this gruesome and pathetic sight, took pity on the dog, and buried him. The jizō saw this and reproached the priest, saying, "Those eighty-eighty crows were the angry souls of the eighty-eight women the dog killed. You should have let them have their revenge; if they had eaten their fill, all the dog's sins would have been expunged and his slate would have been wiped clean. You may have thought it merciful to bury him, but just the contrary: this dog, too, must unavoidably repay his karmic debt. Even if he is hereafter reborn as a man, he will be illness-prone and impoverished, and his whole life will be filled with suffering. He will be, by any measure, a worthless human being."

If you need proof that there ever existed such a dog who was reborn as a human being—here I am. Look no further than my useless legs, which don't even bear my weight. I'm on the floor, crawling on all fours, just like a dog.

10 January 1900

---

[5] This phrase—in Japanese, *nyoze chikushō hotsu bodaishin*—appears also in *Nansō Satomi Hakkenden* (The Chronicles of the Eight Dogs of the Nansō Satomi Clan), a long novel published in 1814-1842 in 106 parts by Kyokutei Bakin (1767–1848).

[6] Pilgrims on the Shikoku trail sometimes pronounce an eight-character invocation to Kōbō-Daishi—the very prayer being howled by the dog here. Kōbō-Daishi (or Taishi) is the posthumous name of the monk Kūkai (774-835 CE), an important figure in early Japanese Buddhism. In representations of his pilgrimage to a famous holy site, Kūkai is sometimes pictured as being accompanied by two dogs.

[7] A *jizō*—in Sanskrit, *kṣitigarbha*—is a guardian deity of travelers and unborn children. In Japan the *jizō* is often represented by a small stone statue, frequently with a red cloth bib.

Rubén Darío

For a Cuban
 — *translated by Chris Campanioni*

Poetry, sweet and mystical, seek the white Cuban woman who leaned out the window as an artistic vision. Mysterious and cabalistic, she can make Diana jealous, with her porcelain form of a Eucharistic whiteness. Full of Asian prestige, red, on the enigmatic face, her scarlet lips pretend and when she smiled I saw in her the brilliance of a star that was the soul of a sphinx.

For the Same
— *translated by Chris Campanioni*

I looked as I sat at the table bathed in the light of day the portrait of
Maria, the Cuban-Japanese. The air caresses and kisses as a lover would
the proud gallantry of thick hair. The Mikado would give a treasure to
feel caressed by such a gentle princess, worthy of being painted by a
great painter next to a flower in an ivory glass.

The Land of the Sun

to a Cuban artist

— translated by Chris Campanioni

Next to the black palace of the king of the island of Iron—(oh, cruel, horrible exile!)—how is it that you, harmonious sister, make the gray sky sing, your birdhouse of nightingales, your formidable box of music? Are you not sad to remember the spring when you heard a divine and brightly-colored bird in the land of the sun? In the garden of the king of the island of Gold—(oh, my dream that I adore!)—I was better than you, harmonious sister, master of your wingéd flutes, your sonorous harps; you who were born where the most beautiful blood carnation and the red rose are born, in the land of the sun! Or in the palace of the queen of the island of Silver (Schubert, sobs the Serenade …) you could also, harmonious sister, make the mystical birds of your soul praise sweetly, very sweetly, the moonlight, the virgin lilies, the nun dove and the marquis swan. The best silver melts in a burning pot, in the land of the sun! Go back, then, to your vessel, which has the sail ready—(it resounds, it lifts, it carries, it flies)—and depart, harmonious sister, to where a beautiful prince, at the seashore, asks for lyres, and verses and roses, and caresses his golden curls under a regal and blue parasol, in the land of the sun!

Ernest Dowson

Absinthia Taetra

Green changed to white, emerald to opal; nothing was changed.
The man let the water trickle gently into his glass, and as the green
clouded, a mist fell from his mind.
Then he drank opaline.

Memories and terrors beset him. The past tore after him like a pan-
ther and through the blackness of the present he saw the luminous
tiger eyes of the things to be.
But he drank opaline.

And that obscure night of the soul, and the valley of humiliation,
through which he stumbled, were forgotten. He saw blue vistas of
undiscovered countries, high prospects and a quiet, caressing sea. The
past shed its perfume over him, to-day held his hand as if it were a
little child, and to-morrow shone like a white star: nothing was
changed.
He drank opaline.

The man had known the obscure night of the soul, and lay even now
in the valley of humiliation; and the tiger menace of the things to be
was red in the skies. But for a little while he had forgotten.
Green changed to white, emerald to opal; nothing was changed.

Paul Claudel

Water's Sadness
— translated by Mary Ann Caws

There is some conceiving in joy, I admit, there is some seeing in laughter. But this mixture of gladness and bitterness implied by the act of creation, so you can understand it, friend, at this time when a somber season is starting, I shall explain to you water's sadness.

From the sky there falls or from the eye there spills an identical tear.

Don't imagine accusing the cloud for your melancholy, nor the dimness of this downpour. Close your eyes and listen! The rain is falling.

Nor does the drone of this constant sound suffice to explain it.

It's the weight of a grief bearing in itself its cause, it's the caring of love, it's the pain of work. The skies are weeping on the earth they are fertilizing. And it's above all not the autumn and the coming fall of the fruit whose seed they nourish that is drawing these tears from the wintry cloud. The pain is summer and the spreading of death in the flower of life.

At the moment when this hour is finishing just before Noon, as I am making my way down into this valley filled by the sound of various fountains, I halt, taken by sorrow. How full of plenty are these waters! And if tears, like blood, have a perpetual source in us, our ear toward this liquid choir of voices abundant or slight, how refreshing it is to match to them all the nuances of its pain! There is no passion which can't borrow its tears from you, oh fountains! And although there is enough for me in the shine of this single drop which from high up in its basin falls upon the image of the moon, I shall not have learned in vain during many afternoons to know of your retreat, vale of sorrow.

Here am I in the plain. On the threshold of this hut, where, in the dark interior there gleams a candle lit for some rustic celebration, a man is seated holding a dusty cymbal. It is raining immensely; and I am hearing, alone, amid this dampened solitude, a goose cry.

Cities

— translated by Michel Delville

Just as there are books on beehives, on cities of birds' nests, or on the constitution of madreporous corals, why should we not study human cities?

Paris, capital of the Kingdom, in its even and concentric development, multiplies, as it grows, the image of the island in which it was once enclosed. London, that juxtaposition of organic parts, stores and produces. New York is a railway terminal; they built houses between tracks, a pier, a jetty flanked by wharves and warehouses; like the tongue which takes and divides its food, like the uvula on the back of the throat between two channels, New York, between its two rivers, the North and the East, has set its docks and depots on Long Island side; on the other, through Jersey City and the twelve railway lines which align their storehouses on the Hudson Embankment, it receives and ships out the merchandise of the whole Western continent; the city's active end, composed entirely of banks, stock exchanges and offices, is like the tip of that tongue which, not to push the metaphor, swings continually from one end to the other. Boston is made of two parts: there is the new city, pedantic and miserly like a man who, displaying his wealth and his virtue, keeps them to himself, as if the cold streets grew more silent and longer, listening with more hatred to the steps of the passerby who follows them, opening up avenues on every side and he, grinding his teeth in the northern wind; and there is the mound of the old town which, like a snail spiral, contains all the unfolding of traffic, debauchery, and hypocrisy. The streets of Chinese cities are made for a people used to walking in single file, each individual takes his place in lines which know no beginning nor end: where fissures have been created between houses resembling boxes with one side kicked in and whose occupants sleep pell-mell among the wares.

Are there not special points to look at? The geometry of streets, the measurements of angles, the mathematics of junctions? Is not all movement parallel to them? And all that is rest or pleasure perpendicular?

A book.

Sidonie-Gabrielle Colette

Dancer's Song
— *translated by Mary Ann Caws*

Calling me a dancer, you should now know that I never learned to dance. You met me when I was small and playful, dancing on the road and chasing before me my blue shadow. I was circling like a bee, and a blonde dusty pollen powdered my feet and hair with a path's color...

You saw me coming back from the fountain, cradling the amphora in my hip's hollow while the water, keeping the rhythm of my steps, leapt up to my tunic like round tears, like silver snakes, in small spurts and frizzes frozen climbing toward my cheek... I was walking slow and serious, but you called my steps a dance. You weren't looking at my face, but following the motion of my knees, the sway of my waist, you were reading on the sand the form of my bare heels, the imprint of my toes that you compared to that of five irregular pearls...

You said to me: "Pick these flowers, follow that butterfly..." for you called my walk a dance, and each bow of my body leaning over the crimson carnations and my gesture, repeated over each flower, of tossing over my shoulder a slippery shawl...

In your house, alone between you and the bright flame of a lamp, you said to me "Dance!" and I didn't dance.

But naked in your arms, tied to your bed by the fiery ribbon of desire, you called me a dancer all the same, seeing the inevitable voluptuousness surge under my skin, from my throat thrown back to my rounded feet...

Tired, I knotted up my hair and you watched it tamed, roll itself around my forehead like some flute-charmed serpent...

I left your house while you were murmuring: "The loveliest of your dances isn't the one when you are running toward me, gasping, full of a desire aroused and already twisting the fastening of your dress, as you come, …It's rather when you are moving away from me, calmed and with your knees weakened, and when, moving away you look at me with your chin on your shoulder…Your body remembers me, wavers and hesitates, your hips miss me and your insides thank me… You look at me, with your head turned, while your feet, aware, feel and choose their path…

"You are going off, still smaller and rosy-toned by the setting sun, until you are no more, atop the slope, so thin in your orange-colored dress, than an upright flame, dancing imperceptibly…"

If you don't leave me, I shall go off, dancing, toward my white tomb.

With an involuntary dance, slowed down every day, I shall salute the light which makes me beautiful and which saw me enlivened.

A last tragic dance will place me in the capture of death, but I shall fight only to succumb gracefully.

May the gods grant me a harmonious fall, my arms joined above my forehead, with one leg folded and the other extended, as if ready to bound lightly over the black threshold of the kingdom of shadows…

You call me a dancer, and yet I don't know how to dance…

Gertrude Stein

A CARAFE, THAT IS A BLIND GLASS.

A kind in glass and a cousin, a spectacle and nothing strange a single hurt color and an arrangement in a system to pointing. All this and not ordinary, not unordered in not resembling. The difference is spreading.

A SUBSTANCE IN A CUSHION.

The change of color is likely and a difference a very little difference is prepared. Sugar is not a vegetable.

Callous is something that hardening leaves behind what will be soft if there is a genuine interest in there being present as many girls as men. Does this change. It shows that dirt is clean when there is a volume.

A cushion has that cover. Supposing you do not like to change, supposing it is very clean that there is no change in appearance, supposing that there is regularity and a costume is that any the worse than an oyster and an exchange. Come to season that is there any extreme use in feather and cotton. Is there not much more joy in a table and more chairs and very likely roundness and a place to put them.

A circle of fine card board and a chance to see a tassel.

What is the use of a violent kind of delightfulness if there is no pleasure in not getting tired of it. The question does not come before there is a quotation. In any kind of place there is a top to covering and it is a pleasure at any rate there is some venturing in refusing to believe nonsense. It shows what use there is in a whole piece if one uses it and it is extreme and very likely the little things could be dearer but in any case there is a bargain and if there is the best thing to do is to take it away and wear it and then be reckless be reckless and resolved on returning gratitude.

Light blue and the same red with purple makes a change. It shows that there is no mistake. Any pink shows that and very likely it is reasonable. Very likely there should not be a finer fancy present. Some increase means a calamity and this is the best preparation for three and more being together. A little calm is so ordinary and in any case there is sweetness and some of that.

A seal and matches and a swan and ivy and a suit.

A closet, a closet does not connect under the bed. The band if it is white and black, the band has a green string. A sight a whole sight and a little groan grinding makes a trimming such a sweet singing trimming and a red thing not a round thing but a white thing, a red thing and a white thing.

The disgrace is not in carelessness nor even in sewing it comes out out of the way.

What is the sash like. The sash is not like anything mustard it is not like a same thing that has stripes, it is not even more hurt than that, it has a little top.

CRANBERRIES.

Could there not be a sudden date, could there not be in the present settlement of old age pensions, could there not be by a witness, could there be.

Count the chain, cut the grass, silence the noon and murder flies. See the basting undip the chart, see the way the kinds are best seen from the rest, from that and untidy.

Cut the whole space into twenty-four spaces and then and then is there a yellow color, there is but it is smelled, it is then put where it is and nothing stolen.

A remarkable degree of red means that, a remarkable exchange is made.

Climbing altogether in when there is a solid chance of soiling no more than a dirty thing, coloring all of it in steadying is jelly.

Just as it is suffering, just as it is succeeded, just as it is moist so is there no countering.

Amy Lowell

Spring Day

Bath

The day is fresh-washed and fair, and there is a smell of tulips and narcissus in the air.

The sunshine pours in at the bath-room window and bores through the water in the bath-tub in lathes and planes of greenish-white. It cleaves the water into flaws like a jewel, and cracks it to bright light.

Little spots of sunshine lie on the surface of the water and dance, dance, and their reflections wobble deliciously over the ceiling; a stir of my finger sets them whirring, reeling. I move a foot, and the planes of light in the water jar. I lie back and laugh, and let the green-white water, the sun-flawed beryl water, flow over me. The day is almost too bright to bear, the green water covers me from the too bright day. I will lie here awhile and play with the water and the sun spots.

The sky is blue and high. A crow flaps by the window, and there is a whiff of tulips and narcissus in the air.

Breakfast Table

In the fresh-washed sunlight, the breakfast table is decked and white. It offers itself in flat surrender, tendering tastes, and smells, and colours, and metals, and grains, and the white cloth falls over its side, draped and wide. Wheels of white glitter in the silver coffee-pot, hot and spinning like catherine-wheels, they whirl, and twirl—and my eyes begin to smart, the little white, dazzling wheels prick them like darts. Placid and peaceful, the rolls of bread spread themselves in the sun to bask. A stack of butter-pats, pyramidal, shout orange through the white, scream, flutter, call: "Yellow! Yellow! Yellow!" Coffee steam rises in a stream, clouds the silver tea-service with mist, and twists up into the sunlight, revolved, involuted, suspiring higher and higher, fluting in a thin spiral up the high blue sky. A crow flies by and croaks at the coffee steam. The day is new and fair with good smells in the air.

Walk

Over the street the white clouds meet, and sheer away without touching.

On the sidewalks, boys are playing marbles. Glass marbles, with amber and blue hearts, roll together and part with a sweet clashing noise. The boys strike them with black and red striped agates. The glass marbles spit crimson when they are hit, and slip into the gutters under rushing brown water. I smell tulips and narcissus in the air, but there are no flowers anywhere, only white dust whipping up the street, and a girl with a gay Spring hat and blowing skirts. The dust and the wind flirt at her ankles and her neat, high-heeled patent leather shoes. Tap, tap, the little heels pat the pavement, and the wind rustles among the flowers on her hat.

A water-cart crawls slowly on the other side of the way. It is green and gay with new paint, and rumbles contentedly, sprinkling clear water over the white dust. Clear zigzagging water, which smells of tulips and narcissus.

The thickening branches make a pink *grisaille* against the blue sky.

Whoop! The clouds go dashing at each other and sheer away just in time. Whoop! And a man's hat careers down the street in front of the white dust, leaps into the branches of a tree, veers away and trundles ahead of the wind, jarring the sunlight into spokes of rose-colour and green.

A motor-car cuts a swathe through the bright air, sharp-beaked, irresistible, shouting to the wind to make way. A glare of dust and sunshine tosses together behind it, and settles down. The sky is quiet and high, and the morning is fair with fresh-washed air.

Midday and Afternoon

Swirl of crowded streets. Shock and recoil of traffic. The stock-still brick façade of an old church, against which the waves of people lurch and withdraw. Flare of sunshine down side-streets. Eddies of light in the windows of chemists' shops, with their blue, gold, purple jars, darting colours far into the crowd. Loud bangs and tremors, murmurings out of high windows, whirring of machine belts, blurring of horses and motors. A quick spin and shudder of brakes on an electric car, and the jar of a church-bell knocking against the metal blue of the sky. I am a piece of the town, a bit of blown dust, thrust along with the crowd. Proud to feel the pavement under me, reeling with feet. Feet tripping, skipping, lagging, dragging, plodding doggedly, or springing up and advancing on firm elastic insteps. A boy is selling papers, I smell them clean and new from the press. They are fresh like the air, and pungent as tulips and narcissus.

The blue sky pales to lemon, and great tongues of gold blind the shop-windows, putting out their contents in a flood of flame.

Night and Sleep

The day takes her ease in slippered yellow. Electric signs gleam out along the shop fronts, following each other. They grow, and grow, and blow into patterns of fire-flowers as the sky fades. Trades scream in spots of light at the unruffled night. Twinkle, jab, snap, that means a new play; and over the way: plop, drop, quiver, is the sidelong sliver of a watchmaker's sign with its length on another street. A gigantic mug of beer effervesces to the atmosphere over a tall building, but the sky is high and has her own stars, why should she heed ours?

I leave the city with speed. Wheels whirl to take me back to my trees and my quietness. The breeze which blows with me is fresh-washed and clean, it has come but recently from the high sky. There are no flowers in bloom yet, but the earth of my garden smells of tulips and narcissus.

My room is tranquil and friendly. Out of the window I can see the distant city, a band of twinkling gems, little flower-heads with no stems. I cannot see the beer-glass, nor the letters of the restaurants and shops I passed, now the signs blur and all together make the city, glowing on a night of fine weather, like a garden stirring and blowing for the Spring.

The night is fresh-washed and fair and there is a whiff of flowers in the air.

Wrap me close, sheets of lavender. Pour your blue and purple dreams into my ears. The breeze whispers at the shutters and mutters queer tales of old days, and cobbled streets, and youths leaping their horses down marble stairways. Pale blue lavender, you are the colour of the sky when it is fresh-washed and fair … I smell the stars … they are like tulips and narcissus … I smell them in the air.

Rainer Maria Rilke

The Lion Cage
— *translated by Michel Delville*

She goes back and forth like the guards standing at the edge of the walls, where there is nothing left. And as in the guards, there is home-sickness in her, a heavy homesickness that comes in segments.

As somewhere down in the sea there must be mirrors, mirrors from the cabins of sunken ships, pieces of mirrors which of course no longer contain anything: not the faces of the travelers, not one of their gestures; not the way they turned and looked so strangely awkward from behind; not the wall, not the corner where they slept; even less what shines, careening in from over there and outside; nothing, no. But maybe like a piece of alga perhaps, an open, sinking octopus, the sudden face of a fish or even just the water itself, which draws, divides and recombines watery resemblances in those mirrors, distant, twisted, false, soon forsaken resemblances with that which was once—:

Thus memories, pieces of memories, lie fractured in the darkness at the bottom of her blood.

She goes back and forth around him, the lion who is ill. Being ill doesn't concern him and doesn't diminish him; it just imprisons him. The way he lies on the floor, the soft inturned paws purposeless, the haughty face covered with a worn-out mane, the unloaded eyes, he has erected upon himself a monument to his own grief, just as he once embodied (always beyond himself) the hyperbole of his own power.

Now it still twitches here and there in the muscles and tautens itself, here and there small spots of anger form, too distant from one another; the blood bursts out angrily, in a leap, from the ventricles, and certainly it has retained the carefully tested twists of resolute suddenness when it enters the brain. But he just lets it happen, because it is not over yet, and does nothing more than withdraw from the world. Only from afar, as if held away from himself, he paints again and again with the soft brush of his tail a small, semicircular gesture of indescribable disdain. And this gesture becomes so significant that the lioness stops and looks over: alarmed, aroused, expectant.

But then she begins moving along again, to the bleak, ridiculous pacing of the sentinel, which falls back into the same footsteps, again and again. She walks and walks back and forth, and sometimes her scattered mask appears, round and full, crossed out by the grid bars.

She goes like clocks go. And on her face, like a dial lit up at night, a strange, unusually briefly shown hour stands: a terrifying hour in which someone dies.

Kanbara Ariake

A Storm
— *translated by Scott Mehl*

Clouds were building. A storm was imminent.

I was reading desultorily in a book of tales of the floating world, written by Saikaku in his Dutch style. I skimmed them without tasting deeply.

My lethargy was such that the book slipped from my hand; whereupon the sensation at the ends of my fingertips became blank and blunted, as if I were feeling my way in a fog, and I heard a sound as of something softening and liquefying.

When I looked to see what could be causing these sensations, I saw that a vapor was rising from the surface of my rosewood desk, like the fumes that escape an open vial of nitric acid.

On this summer afternoon the humidity caused the vegetation to wither and droop, bringing the plants' green-smelling breath to a standstill; little by little their aroma, rich and heady, permeated the room.

The etherized summer day reminded me of nothing so much as an old well that has been sealed off. But the air was not dank and clammy as one would find in such a well; instead, the air was sultry, smelling of decay, laden with eerie sighs.

In my tired brain there came and went images of the beautiful women in Saikaku's tales: they smiled at me, even as they lamented life's gossamer insubstantiality. The red striped linings of their kimono fluttered and waved. I tried to follow the women with my eyes, but my eyelids kept falling shut.

And then I recalled the character Saikaku wrote of, the man who donated brilliantine to the courtesan for her hair. Before my eyes there appeared a great bronze vessel filled with hair oil, glinting and lustrous. A supple hand—just the sort of hand suitable for bringing to such a place a small, shallow porcelain dish of hair oil—enclosed around my hand. This pale, beguiling hand was as cool to the touch as a snake, yet it made me burn all over with longing.

Distractedly, I reached for the old hair-oil container that I'd kept at my desk. It was a small vase, patterned in bright blues and reds: one of the items my curious mind had conserved from the detritus of my past. In moments of tedium I would hold the opening of this little vase under my nose and inhale the perfume. The smooth skin of the porcelain retained, as it had done for so long, a faint fragrance of the familiar oil, whispering a wordless song of obsession.

Gradually I shook off these fevered dreams. The broad leaves of the banana plant, almost as high as the eaves of the house, was swaying vigorously. A wilting bamboo palm, its rachis perfectly perpendicular to the ground, broke off and came tumbling to earth.

Then there came the sound, penetratingly loud, of heavy raindrops falling on the awning over the balcony, and I began surfacing from my dreams of Saikaku's floating world.

A rumble of distant thunder called to mind the smell of asphalt—a smell that harmonized well with that of dry earth absorbing rain.

Then the rain started falling as if crazed, at the very moment when the wind picked up, whipping up the thin branches of the zelkova.

Mustering their strength, my drowsy eyelids snapped open.

And a spray of silver-gray, greenish rain took possession of a darkened world.

Then the storm passed.

After the rain let up, I gave no further thought to Saikaku or to the vessel full of brilliantine, such delight did I find in the flowers I was growing in my celadon pots: jasmine, which opens its white buds when evening comes.

On the top rail of the shoji screen, a fly awaited the all-clear; outside, a cicada keened.

Max Jacob

The Merry Joker
— *translated by Rosanna Warren*

It's me, the merry joker.

The smallest pince-nez on a mustache stops me in my tracks, and not
to find my name on a letter not addressed to me surprises and
wounds me. But if someone organizes a farandole, I know how to
sing and run at the same time. The other day, I was singing "The Little
Hunchback" in a farandole and I noticed there was a hunchback
there. I wondered if I should stop the song or continue it. I had the
wit not to sing all the verses. It's me, the merry joker.

from *Le Cornet à dés.*
Extracts from Section IV
— *translated by Rosanna Warren*

You're going out? Everyone will see that you're sick: the castor-
lanterns are observing you and the seesaw zebra makes you dizzy.

*

I declare myself worldwide, oviparous, a giraffe, thirsty, sinophobic and
hemispherical. I drink from the sources of the atmosphere which
laughs concentrically and farts at my ineptitude.

*

His white arms became my whole horizon.

*

A burning house is a rose on a peacock's open tail.

*

When you paint a picture, at each touch, it entirely changes; it turns
like a cylinder and it seems almost interminable. When it stops turning,
it's finished. My last one represented a Tower of Babel as lit candles.

*

When you snore, the material world wakes the other.

*

Going down the rue de Rennes, I bit into my bread with so much
feeling I thought it was my heart I was tearing open.

★

The archangel struck by lightning only had time to loosen his necktie; it looked as if he were still praying.

★

So do they think a man has truffles in his heart?

★

Mystery is in this life, reality in the other; if you love me, if you love me, I'll show you reality.

★

I bring you my two sons said the old acrobat to the Virgin of the Ricks who was playing the mandolin. The younger one knelt in his cute little suit; the other carried a fish at the end of a rod.

Sherwood Anderson

The Cornfields

I am pregnant with song. My body aches but do not betray me. I will sing songs and hide them away. I will tear them into bits and throw them in the street. The streets of my city are full of dark holes. I will hide my songs in the holes of the streets.

In the darkness of the night I awoke and the bands that bind me were broken. I was determined to bring old things into the land of the new. A sacred vessel I found and ran with it into the fields, into the long fields where the corn rustles.

All of the people of my time were bound with chains. They had forgotten the long fields and the standing corn. They had forgotten the west winds.

Into the cities my people had gathered. They had become dizzy with words. Words had choked them. They could not breathe.

On my knees I crawled before my people. I debased myself.

The excretions of their bodies I took for my food. Into the ground I went and my body died. I emerged in the corn, in the long cornfields. My head arose and was touched by the west wind. The light of old things, of beautiful old things, awoke in me. In the cornfields the sacred vessel is set up.

I will renew in my people the worship of gods. I will set up for a king before them. A king shall arise before my people. The sacred vessel shall be filled with the sweet oil of the corn.

The flesh of my body is become good. With your white teeth you may bite me. My arm that was withered has become strong. In the quiet night streets of my city old things are awake.

I awoke and the bands that bind me were broken. I was determined to bring love into the hearts of my people. The sacred vessel was put into my hands and I ran with it into the fields. In the long cornfields the sacred vessel is set up.

Song of Industrial America

They tell themselves so many little lies, my beloved. Now wait, little one we can't sing. We are standing in a crowd, by a bridge, in the West. Hear the voices turn around let's go home I am tired. They tell themselves so many little lies.

You remember in the night we arose. We were young. There was smoke in the passage and you laughed. Was it good that black smoke? Look away to the streams and the lake. We're alive. See my hand how it trembles on the rail.

Here is song, here in America, here now, in our time. Now wait I'll go to the train. I'll not swing off into tunes. I'm all right I just want to talk.

You watch my hand on the rail of this bridge. I press down. The blood goes down there. That steadies me it makes me all right.

Now here's how it's going to come the song, I mean. I've watched things, men and faces I know.

First there are the broken things myself and the others. I don t mind that I'm gone shot to pieces. I'm part of the scheme I'm the broken end of a song myself. We are all that, here in the West, here in Chicago. Tongues clatter against teeth. There's nothing but shrill screams and a rattle. That had to be it's a part of the scheme.

Elena Guro

A Newspaper Advertisement
— *translated by Matvei Yankelevich*

Especially warm camel down jerseys,

underpants, tights, and belly-warmers

It is done as follows: they ambush and capture good spirits, kind ones, on the tall side, that look like lanky golden baby camels, covered in the down of divine light. Then they drive a bunch of these together, whips snapping about the air, and the tender good hearted creatures, too kind, really, to understand how is it that pain is made, crowd together tightly, each extending a neck over another, pressing themselves against the crude fence, shedding their tender down in the crush.

And it's this down of the baby camels of the sky that warms with its spring-time, life-bearing warmth, that they pick up off the ground and from it weave jerseys.

"And what about the poor baby camels, will they kill them just like that?" they asked me in some distress.

"Why, there's no need to kill them. They'll drive them for a while until all the down comes off and then let them go back into the sky until the next time. And their down will grow back in no more than a minute, even better than the last."

Snowpuddles of the Sky
— translated by Matvei Yankelevich

Unbearably clean and faraway, the stripes grew more northerly.

Amid the clouds, the lakes swam all day, so much like proud swans in azure.
Amid the black birches lived a heavenly snowpuddle, and it breathed.

It breathed and the birches were moist.

From up high, messengers walked on the heavenly snowpuddles, passing through across the whole slant-leaning sky. And their steps were heard only by the proud souls of the trees, enlightened by the deep hollows of the firmaments, and towers understood by none.

And the tender fallen sky that let its caressing palms down to the earth.

And they strode across the sky, near to the earth as it was, humble in its clarity, the sky that had become tender and singed, long steadfast by the earth's side. Little twigs, saddened by urban proximity, swayed there in the sky. Tram after tram flew racing by, taking notice of the little twigs.

The messengers strode on, and the enlightened souls of remotely distanced hills and towers heard them stride.

And those already manifested heard them — and prayed.

And somewhere lakes stretched out, lake upon lake, extending.

When a youth is walking to meet the north, the wind beats directly on his forehead, his clean, open forehead that knew not yet how to fear.

His hair flying like a horse's forelock. And a horse's speed to him who is ahead, and there, ahead like lakes upon lakes.

Somewhere too, during those days, a porch step was melting, and over and above it a larch spread its branches like a fir tree. And the larch breathed.

★★ ★ ★★
   — *translated by Matvei Yankelevich*

And the one said, "we're completing it." And the other said, "I believe it."

And neither the friend nor all the friends would say, "so deep it was, so deeply pink was the sky."

And the passerby approached, saying, "friend."

And that of the slowly freezing, evening barns said, "friend."

He stopped and said: "I believe, I believe you."

"Come in!"

"No, I'm in a hurry. I'm hurrying, but I believe." The roads ran off through the universe in all directions, not responding to each other, nor calling out.

So deep, so deep was the pink sky.

So pink, as if a spoken covenant, it worried the soul, and the words blossomed and reached all the way to the very lips, and then, without falling, they fizzled out in a half-question and could not be torn away, and blossomed again.

It seems as if someone was walking, signaling proudly to the audaciously proud men that hurtled, with winged steps and gestures, toward the oncoming stream of days.

Spring, Spring!

— *translated by Matvei Yankelevich*

What a funny little camel he was—so diligent. He studied so hard for the exams and then, bashfully, with eccentricity, he flunked completely. And at every dawn, rather than snuggle with his nose in a pillow… furtively, secretly, he penned poems.

He let his assiduous studies deny him the joy of first leaves in spring sky. But, though he would have felt so much more comfortable around strangers, he simply wasn't capable of keeping his pants from sticking out over his belt, his shirt from hanging like a sack.

He did not know how to make it known he had no desire to play tennis—and everyone saw that his bashfulness made him unable to play, and also they saw his desire to hide his bashfulness, and that he couldn't do that either, while he knew, painfully, that on his very back they could read just how unbearably awkward he felt… And so, he saw merriment most often as retreating, moving away from him, or flickering in the far distance between the trees.

And yet on the bottom of mirror-still lakes one can glimpse unsullied dawns of cranes. Solitary, pure vaults of sky.

When the little camel looked at the sky, in the rosy sky his warm and native land unfurled.

Promise It

— *translated by Matvei Yankelevich*

Swear to it, distant ones and near ones, you who write with ink on paper, with your gaze on clouds, paint on canvas, swear never to betray or slander that beautiful, ephemeral creation — the face of your reverie, be it friendship or faith in people or in your own songs.

Reverie! — you've let it live; now it lives — already this creation does not belong to us, just as already we do not belong to ourselves.

Swear it, especially you who write your gaze on the clouds — the clouds change shape — it is so easy to defile with faithlessness their day-old visage.

Promise it, please! Promise it to life, promise it to me!

Promise!

Renée Vivien

The Black Swan
— translated by Mary Ann Caws

Over the weighty waves drifted a cloud of bright swans. They left a silver reflection in their wake.

Seen far off, they seemed a snow. But one day they perceived a black swan whose odd aspect ruined the harmony of their gathered whiteness.

He had funereal feathers and a beak of bleeding red.

The swans took fright at their strange companion.

Their terror became hatred and they so badly besieged the black swan that he nigh perished.

And the black swan said to himself "I'm tired of the cruelty of my lookalikes who are not my equals."

"I'm tired of the hushed enmities and the declared angers."

"I'll flee forever in the vast solitudes."

"I'll soar up and fly off towards the sea."

"I'll know the taste of the bitterACRE breezes of wide space LARGE and the voluptuousness of the tempest."

"The tumultuous waves will rock my slumber, and I shall rest in the storm."

"Lightning shall be my mysterious sister, and thunder, my beloved brother."

He soared up and flew towards the sea.

The peace of the fjords did not hold him, and he never lingered by the unreal reflections of the trees and the grass; he disdained the austere unmoving-ness of mountains.

He listened to the faraway rhythm of the waves rustling...

But, one day, the hurricane caught him by surprise and forced him down and broke his wings...

The black swan dimly understood he would die without having seen the sea...

And yet, he savored in the air the smell of distance...

The wind brought him a taste of salt and the seaweed's aphrodisiac perfume...

His broken wings lifted in a last burst of love

And the wind carried his cadaver toward the sea.

Victor Segalen

Mongol Libation
— translated by Roger Célestin

This is where we caught him alive. Since he fought well we offered him our ranks: he preferred to serve his Prince unto death.

We cut his hamstrings: he shook his arms to show his zeal. We cut his arms: he screamed out his devotion to Him.

We slit his mouth from ear to ear: he signaled, with his eyes, that he remained faithful still.

Let us not gouge out his eyes, as to a coward; but, cutting off his head with respect, pour the koumiss of the brave, and this libation:

When you will be reborn, Tch'en Houo-chang, grant us the honor of being reborn among us.

Stela of Tears
— translated by Roger Célestin

If you are man, read no further: the pain I carry is so vast and somber it would stifle your heart.

If you are Chenn, turn away even faster: the horror I point to will make you as heavy as my stone.

If you are woman, boldly read me to burst into laughter, and forever forget to stop laughing.

But if you are a eunuch at the Palace, confront me without danger or resentment, and keep the secret I utter.

Lord Dunsany

The Giant Poppy

I dreamt that I went back to the hills I knew, whence on a clear day you can see the walls of Ilion and the plains of Roncesvalles. There used to be woods along the tops of those hills with clearings in them where the moonlight fell, and there when no one watched the fairies danced.

But there were no woods when I went back, no fairies nor distant glimpse of Ilion or plains of Roncesvalles, only one giant poppy waved in the wind, and as it waved it hummed "Remember not." And by its oak-like stem a poet sat, dressed like a shepherd and playing an ancient tune softly upon a pipe. I asked him if the fairies had passed that way or anything olden.

He said: "The poppy has grown apace and is killing gods and fairies. Its fumes are suffocating the world, and its roots drain it of its beautiful strength." And I asked him why he sat on the hills I knew, playing an olden tune.

And he answered: "Because the tune is bad for the poppy, which would otherwise grow more swiftly; and because if the brotherhood of which I am one were to cease to pipe on the hills men would stray over the world and be lost or come to terrible ends. We think we have saved Agamemnon."

Then he fell to piping again that olden tune, while the wind among the poppy's sleepy petals murmured "Remember not. Remember not."

Lu Xun

Epitaph
— *translated by Nick Admussen*

I dreamed I stood opposite a tomb's stone tablet, reading the words carved into it. It seemed to be of sandstone, much had crumbled away and clumps of moss grew all over it. Only some of its text had survived —

....*shivering during the fever of the soaring anthem; watching the heavens and seeing the abyss. Looking into the nothingness inside all eyes; in hopelessness, being saved....*

....*a wandering spirit that turned into a serpent, its mouth full of venomous teeth. No person as prey, it eats itself, head swallowed at last....*

....*leave!....*

I walked around the tablet, and only behind it did I see the lonely grave. No grass grew on it, but it was already deteriorating. Then through a large crack, I saw the corpse, chest completely caved in, no heart, no liver. On its face, no mark of joy or pain, instead there was a drizzle as fine as mist.

In my apprehension, I turned around a moment after I should have, and saw a remnant of text on the shadowy side of the stone tablet:

....*to tear out the heart and eat it, greedy to know the depth of its flavor. The pain's so fierce, how can the flavor be tasted?....*

....*the pain subsides, the meal begins. But the heart has gone stale, how now can its real savor be known?....*

....*answer me. Otherwise, leave!....*

I did want to leave. But the corpse had sat up in its grave, its lips and tongue motionless, it spoke —

Wait until I turn to dust, then you'll see my smile!

I bolted, didn't dare look back, I was terrified to see him following.

James Joyce

from Giacomo Joyce

Who? A pale face surrounded by heavy odorous furs.
Her movements are shy and nervous. She uses quizzing-
glasses.
Yes: a brief syllable. A brief laugh. A brief beat of the
eyelids.

★

The lady goes aspace, aspace, aspace ... ...Pure air on the upland road.
Trieste is waking rawly: raw sunlight over its huddled browntiled
roofs, testudoform; a multitude of prostrate bugs await a national
deliverance. Bellumo rises from the bed of his wife's lover's wife: the
busy housewife is astir, sloe-eyed, a saucer of acetic acid in her hand
... ...Pure air and silence on the upland road: and hoofs. A girl on
horseback. Hedda! Hedda Gabler!

★

She raises her arms in an effort to hook at the nape of her neck a
gown of black veiling. She cannot: no, she cannot. She moves back-
wards towards me mutely. I raise my arms to help her: her arms fall. I
hold the websoft edges of her gown and drawing them out to hook
them I see through the opening of the black veil her lithe body
sheathed in an orange shift. It slips its ribbons of moorings at her
shoulders and falls slowly: a lithe smooth naked body shimmering
with silvery scales. It slips slowly over the slender buttocks of smooth
polished silver and over their furrow, a tarnished silver shadow ....
Fingers, cold and calm and moving .... A touch, a touch.

★

A ricefield near Vercelli under creamy summer haze. The wings of her drooping hat shadow her false smile. Shadows streak her falsely smiling face, smitten by the hot creamy light, grey wheyhued shadows under the jawbones, streaks of eggyolk yellow on the moistened brow, rancid yellow humour lurking within the softened pulp of the eyes

★

The sellers offer on their altars the first fruits: green-flecked lemons, jeweled cherries, shameful peaches with torn leaves. The carriage passes through the lane of canvas stalls, its wheel spokes spinning in the glare. Make way! Her father and his son sit in the carriage. They have owls' eyes and owls' wisdom. Owlish wisdom stares from their eyes brooding upon the lore of their *Summa contra Gentiles*.

★

In the raw veiled spring morning faint odours float of morning Paris: aniseed, damp sawdust, hot dough of bread: and as I cross the Pont Saint Michel the steel-blue waking waters chill my heart. They creep and lap about the island whereon men have lived since the stone age ... ...Tawny gloom in the vast gargoyled church. It is cold as on that morning: *quia frigus erat*. Upon the steps of the far high altar, naked as the body of the Lord, the ministers lie prostrate in weak prayer. The voice of an unseen reader rises, intoning the lesson from Hosea. *Haec dicit Dominus: in tribulation sua mane consurgent ad me. Venite et revertamur ad Dominum* ... She stands beside me, pale and chill, clothed with the shadows of the sindark nave, her thin elbow at my arm. Her flesh recalls the thrill of that raw mist-veiled morning, hurrying torches, cruel eyes. Her soul is sorrowful, trembles and would weep. Weep not for me, O daughter of Jerusalem!

★

Loggione. The sodden walls ooze a steamy damp. A symphony of smells fuses the mass of huddled human forms: sour reek of armpits, nozzled oranges, melting breast ointments, mastick water, the breath of suppers of sulphurous garlic, foul phosphorescent farts, opoponax, the frank sweat of marriageable and married womankind, the soapy stink of men ... ... All night I have watched her, all night I shall see her: braided and pinnacled hair and olive oval face and calm soft eyes. A green fillet upon her hair and about her body a green-broidered gown: the hue of the illusion of the vegetable glass of nature and of lush grass, the hair of graves.

Virginia Woolf

Blue and Green

Green

THE POINTED FINGERS of glass hang downwards. The light slides down the glass, and drops a pool of green. All day long the ten fingers of the lustre drop green upon the marble. The feathers of parakeets– their harsh cries–sharp blades of palm trees–green, too; green needles glittering in the sun. But the hard glass drips on to the marble; the pools hover above the desert sand; the camels lurch through them; the pools settle on the marble; rushes edge them; weeds clog them; here and there a white blossom; the frog flops over; at night the stars are set there unbroken. Evening comes, and the shadow sweeps the green over the mantlepiece; the ruffled surface of ocean. No ships come; the aimless waves sway beneath the empty sky. It's night; the needles drip blots of blue. The green's out.

Blue

The snub-nosed monster rises to the surface and spouts through his blunt nostrils two columns of water, which, fiery-white in the centre, spray off into a fringe of blue beads. Strokes of blue line the black tarpaulin of his hide. Slushing the water through mouth and nostrils he sings, heavy with water, and the blue closes over him dowsing the polished pebbles of his eyes. Thrown upon the beach he lies, blunt, obtuse, shedding dry blue scales. Their metallic blue stains the rusty iron on the beach. Blue are the ribs of the wrecked rowing boat. A wave rolls beneath the blue bells. But the cathedral's different, cold, incense laden, faint blue with the veils of madonnas.

Mina Loy

O MARCEL ... OTHERWISE
I ALSO HAVE BEEN TO LOUISE'S

I don't like a lady in evening dress, salting. From here she has black eyes, no mouth, some—Will you bring a perfection, well bring a bottle—Two perfections, WELL I want to SEE it—he will know it afterwards—will you bring the bottle? Really, have I? Which way? Oh did I? WHEN? Too much? You are abusing myself. No, you would not—Did you ask Demuth about it? Anything you like, would I? Ough Noaw? Of course not? Yes I do. I used to kill myself with the syphon—. You don't remember that ball. Well don't do that because I am perfectly sober now—that's the kid he looks like—It will probably cost me very much I have not got money. Dis I say I wanted the bottle all right—SEE it! Excuse me, explain it. You don't need any. I will give you some paper Mina and keep silent to give you a rest. Oh! I will give you some paper all the same. Very much. He said to me, we will toss whether you resign or I resign—a very old French story about "the English man must shoot first." She has a pencil in her hair—very impressionistic. You know you should have some salt on your hair it's so nice—because? Nothing—it's music. Ah this is, this is, this is, is IT. Do not worryabout such things as lighting a match. I give you my key Clara—HEY—have some yellow paper. If carried away If Clara ever returns it. Well, you did about a week, after. Here's the salt-ing lady—I will show her to you-salting lady. She passed. Do not speak any more—you have to squeeze it, maid of the—. I used to go every day—waitress. I feel ashamed in front of this girl—she looks at me from far it's wonderful—it's wo - onderFUL!

Yes, have a drink lady, teaspoon by teaspoon. No please take this—Do I eat? You know why I have done—I do—I have it—I want some tongue I will give you some—but don't do too much what? Suck it. Well I don't know how I will get up early tomorrow I have a lesson at two—no not with the "bellemère" You don't know what a wonderful sensation that is—I have some preference for some company where is our waiter—where is he it sounds it doesn't he?

Mina are you short-hand?, I never knew it. I want tongue sandwich, anyway it keeps me awake. You know, she comes riding school fifty sixth street you know she comes. Lunch 12 o'clock. Well you know it was. How do you light a cigarette—how do you light a match? Did you, well it is not dangerous at all—Did you got it? You are Pennsylvania I am Boston. Do you want some cigarettes—Did you put the pronunciation? Waiter! Tongue sandwiches. Do you want hot milk? Two perfections she doesn't want anything—you go it? She can't write it down anyway—through the flag oh some cigarettes—waiter I want some cigarettes for Mina—this is a wonderful tune Ti lis li laera Mina I give you two dollars, it means to me two dollars—Ti li li laera—it is twice I need to shave now. Demuth you must be careful of your key she keeps it about a week every key she gets she keeps. You speak like little Carlo, well when he wants to imitate—well have a drink! You know those two girls are crazy about that man, they mustn't, you must get him out. I will have a tongue sandwich—you must suck it—Censorship! Don't let your flag get wet—is that Billy Sunday—There's always a sky in heaven!—that is too low. My ancestor is tall people. Don't write, he is going to leave you for a minute. Sandwiches—Oh I forgot to telephone—what shall I say? Ti li li laere—she said—all right!

Franz Kafka

At Night
— translated by Michel Delville

Lost in the night. Just as sometimes you bow your head to think, so completely lost in the night. All around people are asleep. A little play-acting, an innocent self-deception that they sleep in houses, in solid beds, under solid roofs, stretched out or huddled on mattresses, in sheets, under blankets; in reality they have gathered as they did in the past and then again later in a desolate area, an outdoor camp, countless numbers of men, an army, a whole people under a cold sky, on the cold earth, thrown to the ground where they once stood, their foreheads pressing on their arms, their faces against the earth, breathing calmly. And you are watching, you are one of the watchmen, you see the next one in the light of the burning stick you clutched from the pile of brushwood at your feet. Why are you watching? Someone must watch, it is said. Someone has to do it.

Mizuno Yōshū

Peonies
— translated by Scott Mehl

Flowers... Within the maelstrom of evaporation that has formed in the greenhouse, among all the green of the leaves unfurled by the profusion of grasses and trees, crimson peonies are inhaling and exhaling. The air they breathe comes out hot. They quiver and shudder, in a state of constant agitation, their pulse quickening. The peonies seem to be fighting for air... the petals are panting with all the heat they are emitting...

A force of vitality—so pervasive and assertive that it's almost frightening—is causing the air around the peonies to ripple from the heat. The flowers seem almost bewildered, so insistently do they tremble with thermal energy. In the face of all these passions, the flowers have no margin for self-awareness: time simply passes in a blaze of heat.

With their nerves at so elevated a temperature, the force of their rapt attention to their own vitality is the only force in the cosmos that exerts any influence over the petals. And when the rays of the sun fall on them, the solar energy finds a sympathetic response in the energy coming from within the peonies themselves.

But when darkness smothers the panes of glass that form the roof of the greenhouse, the flowers hear, using their ears, the vibrations caused by their warmth. It is agonizing. It is hard to breathe. It hurts to breathe.

★

The moments go painfully by, bringing ever worse torments.

The petals are heavy. They are bursting with moisture, quivering in the constant circulation of the saturated air inside the greenhouse. With rays of light streaming in through the glass, the sun breathes its stifling hot breath upon the flowers.

At even a short distance from these flowers, though, there is no hint of a rainbow-hued dream. There is only a cold mist. Nor are there any of those apparitions such as early summer air would let one have a vision of, a vision in which shadow and variegated colors would mingle brilliantly. Beyond the panes of glass, all that can be seen is the towering, moistureless winter sky, pale and ashen.

Below the glass, unaware of any of these things, the crimson peonies open their eyes, transpiring hotly.

Such beauty belongs to these flowers in their heedless heat, dyed the madman's hue!

★

The nighttime is terrifying; the night stabs deeper and deeper into the flowers' skin.

Within the darkness that smothers the roof of the greenhouse, there is a chill so dry that it stings. The agony… A pain as of pinpricks causes the petals to recoil that had been breathing so hotly. The pain begins its assault upon the flowers. And with each cold stab of the needle, the flowers shudder; they can bear no more. With each second that passes, the very form of time is made visible. The flowers can feel time beating its rhythm every hundredth of a second, nay even every thousandth of a second.

The peonies will die. Yes, the crimson peonies will soon be dead. These flowers, which had lived by force of warmth alone, will die…

Arturo Giovannitti

The Bankrupt's Suicide

He lay in the silver-and-blue boudoir in the royal suite of the great hotel, full-stretched on the shimmering rug, a thin asp of black blood creeping down from his left nostril; his bog hands open, giving back everything—his dream, his gold and his gun.

He had played the game manfully and fiercely and he had lost; and now he lay there as a last payment in full to the little mob that had come to cash his promise.

And the little mob that had been bought free by the blood of fools and had taken alms from the hands of beggars, waited for the scavengers of the law to turn out the pockets of this last monger of salvations who has failed for ten million dollars.

They glowered at him, their faces as vile with anger and as red as the buttocks of mandrills—chocked with a sullen fury against death that had cheated them of their revenge;

Yet were he alive, could he but rise again, they would grovel before him and still acclaim the magic of his words and still pray that the alchemy of his brain turn their inanity into gold, their cowardice into power.

Scientist

You have said Amen to all unexpected truths: You have broken
through and brought down the arches of the eternal incantations of
Nature, giving names and features and scopes and actions to their
dismembered debris, making equal in the distinction of their separate
lineage the spine of a steel wheel to the framework of the Universe;
the dregs of a chemical precipitate to the astral coze of the Milky Way;
the pollen of the edelweiss on the brow of Mount Blanc to the
dandruff on the gown of the Lord Chief Justice.

Aye, and of a monkey you made man.

The Walker

I hear footsteps over my head all night.
They come and they go. Again they come and they go all night.
They come one eternity in four paces and they go one eternity in
four paces, and between the coming and the going there is
silence and the Night and the Infinite.
For infinite are the nine feet of a prison cell, endless is the march
    of him who walks between the yellow brick wall and the red
    iron gate, thinking things that cannot be chained and cannot
    be locked, but that wander far away in the sunlit world, each
    in a wild pilgrimage after a destined goal.

Throughout the restless night I hear the footsteps over my head,
Who walks? I know not. It is the phantom of the jail, the sleepless
    brain, a man, the man, the Walker.
One-two-three-four: four paces and the wall.
One-two-three-four: four paces and the iron gate.
He has measured his pace, he has measured it accurately, scrupulously,
    minutely, as the hangman measures the rope and the
    gravedigger the coffin – so many feet, so many inches so
    many fractions of an inch for each of the four paces.
One-two-three-four. Each step sounds heavy and hollow over my
    head, and the echo of each step sounds hollow within my head
    as I count them in suspense and in dread that once, perhaps, in
    the endless walk, there may be five steps instead of four
    between the yellow brick wall and the red iron gate.
But he has measured the space so accurately, so scrupulously, so
    minutely that nothing breaks the grave rhythm of the slow,
    fantastic march.

When All are asleep, (and who knows but I when all sleep?) three
    things are still awake in the night. The Walker, my heart
    and the old clock which has the soul of a fiend – for never,

since a coarse hand with red hair on its fingers swung for
the first time the pendulum in the jail, has the old clock tick-
tocked a full hour of joy.

Yet the old clock which marks everything and records everything,
and to everything tolls the death knell, the wise old
clock that knows everything, does not know the number of
the footsteps of the Walker nor the throbs of my heart.

For not for the Walker, nor for my heart is there a second, a
minute, an hour or anything that is in the old clock — there
is nothing but the night, the sleepless night, the watchful
night, and footsteps that go, and footsteps that come and the
wild, tumultuous beatings that trail after them forever.

All the sounds of the living beings and inanimate things, and all
the voices and all the noises of the night I have heard in my
wistful vigil.
I have heard the moans of him who bewails a thing that is dead
and the sighs of him who tries to smother a thing that will
not die;
I have heard the stifled sobs of the one who weeps with his head
under the coarse blankets, and the whisperings of the one
who prays with his forehead on the hard, cold stone of the
floor;
I have beard him who laughs the shrill sinister laugh of folly at
the horror rampant on the yellow wall and at the red eyes
of the nightmare glaring through the iron bars;
I have heard in the sudden icy silence him who coughs a dry
ringing cough and wished madly that his throat would not
rattle so and that he would not spit on the floor, for no sound
was more atrocious than that of his sputum upon the floor;
I have heard him who swears fearsome oaths which I listen to in
reverence and awe, for they are holier than the virgin's
prayer;

And I have heard, most terrible of all, the silence of two hundred
    brains all possessed by one single, relentless, unforgiving
    desperate thought.
All this have I heard in the watchful night,
    And the murmur of the wind beyond the walls,
    And the tolls of a distant bell,
    And the woeful dirge of the rain
And the remotest echoes of the sorrowful city
And the terrible beatings, wild beatings, mad beatings of the One
    Heart which is nearest to my heart.

All this have I heard in the still night;
But nothing is louder, harder, drearier, mightier or more awful than
    the footsteps I hear over my head all night.

Yet fearsome and terrible are all the footsteps of men upon this
    earth, for they either descend or climb.
They descend from little mounds and high peaks and lofty altitudes
    through wide roads and narrow paths, down noble marble
    stairs and creaky stairs of wood - and some go down to the
    cellar, and some to the grave, and some down to the pits of
    shame and infamy, and still come to the glory of an unfathom-
    able abyss where there is nothing but the staring white, stony
    eyeballs of Destiny.
And again other footsteps climb. They climb to life and to love,
    to fame, to power, to vanity, to truth, to glory and to the
    scaffold – to everything but Freedom and the Ideal.
And they all climb the same roads and the same stairs others go
    down; for never, since man began to think how to overcome
    and overpass man, have other roads and other stairs been
    found.
They descend and they climb, the fearful footsteps of men, and
    some limp, some drag, some speed, some trot, some run –

they are quiet, slow, noisy, brisk, quick, feverish, mad, and
  most awful is their cadence to the ears of the one who stands
  still.
But of all the footsteps of men that either descend or climb, no
  footsteps are so fearsome and terrible as those that go straight
  on the dead level of a prison floor, from a yellow stone wall
  to a red iron gate.

All through the night he walks and he thinks. Is it more frightful
  because he walks and his footsteps sound hollow over my
  head, or because he thinks and speaks not his thoughts?
But does he think? Why should he think? Do I think? I only hear
  the footsteps and count them. Four steps and the wall. Four
  steps and the gate. But beyond? Beyond? Where goes he
  beyond the gate and the wall?

He goes not beyond. His thought breaks there on the iron gate
  Perhaps it breaks like a wave of rage, perhaps like a sudden
  flood of hope, but it always returns to beat the wall like a
  billow of helplessness and despair.
He walks to and fro within the narrow whirlpit of this ever storming
  and furious thought. Only one thought – constant, fixed
  immovable, sinister without power and without voice.
A thought of madness, frenzy, agony and despair, a hellbrewed
  thought, for it is a natural thought. All things natural are
  things impossible while there are jails in the world – bread,
  work, happiness, peace, love.
But he thinks not of this. As he walks he thinks of the most superhuman,
  the most unattainable, the most impossible thing in
  the world:
He thinks of a small brass key that turns just half around and
  throws open the red iron gate.

That is all the Walker thinks, as he walks throughout the night.

And that is what two hundred minds drowned in the darkness and
the silence of the night think, and that is also what I think.

Wonderful is the supreme wisdom of the jail that makes all think
the same thought. Marvelous is the providence of the law
that equalizes all, even, in mind and sentiment. Fallen is the
last barrier of privilege, the aristocracy of the intellect.

The democracy of reason has leveled all the two hundred minds
to the common surface of the same thought.

I, who have never killed, think like the murderer;

I, who have never stolen, reason like the thief;

I think, reason, wish, hope, doubt, wait like the hired assassin
the embezzler, the forger, the counterfeiter, the incestuous,
the raper, the drunkard, the prostitute, the pimp, I, I who
used to think of love and life and flowers and song and
beauty and the ideal.

A little key, a little key as little as my little finger, a little key of
shining brass.

All my ideas, my thoughts, my dreams are congealed in a little
key of shiny brass.

All my brain, all my soul, all that suddenly surging latent power
of my deepest life are in the pocket of a white-haired man
dressed in blue.

He is great, powerful, formidable, the man with the white hair,
for he has in his pocket the mighty talisman which makes
one man cry, and one man pray, and one laugh, and one
cough, and one walk, and all keep awake and listen and think
the same maddening thought.

Greater than all men is the man with the white hair and the small
brass key, for no other man in the world could compel two
hundred men to think for so long the same thought. Surely
when the light breaks I will write a hymn unto him which
shall hail him greater than Mohammed and Arbues and Tor-

quemada and Mesmer, and all the other masters of other
men's thoughts. I shall call him Almighty, for he holds every-
thing of all and of me in a little brass key in his pocket.

Everything of me he holds but the branding iron of contempt and
    the claymore of hatred for the monstrous cabala that can
    make the apostle and the murderer, the poet and the procurer,
    think of the same gate, the same key and the same
    exit on the different sunlit highways of life.

My brother, do not walk any more.
    It is wrong to walk on a grave. It is a sacrilege to walk four
    steps from the headstone to the foot and four steps from the
    foot to the headstone.
If you stop walking, my brother, no longer will this be a grave,
    – for you will give me back my mind that is chained to your
    feet and the right to think my own thoughts.
I implore you, my brother, for I am weary of the long vigil, weary
    of counting your steps, and heavy with sleep.
Stop, rest, sleep, my brother, for the dawn is well nigh and it is
    not the key alone that can throw open the gate.

Dino Campana

from *Orphic Songs*

The Russian
— *translated by Peter Constantine*

The Russian had been condemned. Nineteen months now confined,
starved, relentlessly spied upon, made to confess. Smeared and
tortured! The monks with placid pleasure and the felons with silent
sneers intimated that he had revealed with a word, a gesture, with
wild weeping in the night smidgeon after smidgeon of his secret. I
now watched him cover his ears to shut out the relentless rattling
steps that hissed like pebbles in a stream.

★★★

These were the first days of spring's awakening in Flanders. From the
vaulted cell (the cell where the true lunatics were kept and where I
now had been put), I watched the cornice looming up against the
sunset, beyond the thick window panes, beyond the iron bars. Golden
dust covered the meadows, and far away the silent silhouette of the
town was shattered by gothic towers. It was thus that I greeted the
spring every evening as I went to bed in my prison. And it was on
one of those evenings that I heard that they had killed the Russian.
Suddenly the golden dust that enveloped the city seemed exalted into
a bloody sacrifice. When had they killed him? It was as if the blood-
stained reflections of the sunset were bringing me his greetings. I
closed my eyes, I lay there for a long time, my mind empty of
thoughts. I wanted nothing more that evening. Darkness was descend-
ing. In the cell there was only the stench and the stifled breathing of
the lunatics, asleep after their delusions. With my head sunk in my
pillow I followed a few moths flitting in the cold faint light around
the electric lamp. An acute sweetness, the sweetness of torment, of his

torment, shuddered through my body. Feverish, hunched over by the edge of the stove, the bearded head was writing. His flitting pen screeched in fits and starts. Why had he set himself to save other men? There was a portrait of a felon he had painted, a dull-witted man, severe in his elegant clothes, his head held up high with animal dignity. Another of his portraits, a smile, the image of a smile sketched from memory, the head of Isabella d'Este. The heads of Russian peasants, all of them bearded heads, heads, heads, more heads...

His flitting pen screeched in fits and starts: why had he set out to save other men? Hunched over, his bearded head by the edge of the stove, the Russian wrote and wrote and wrote...

"A Day in a Life of a Neurotic (Bologna)," *Orphic Songs*
— *translated by Marianna Rosen*

The clerical and scholarly old city was shrouded in the fog of a
December afternoon. The hills were unveiling beyond the planes clat-
tered with church bells. Across the tracks the station appeared closer
in a false perspective of leaden light. Shrouded in furs, faded female
figures in immensely romantic hats preened along the promenade;
protruding out of their fleshy boas like birds from a village courtyard,
they drew closer in small automatic tremors. Muffled blows, hisses
from the station intensify monotony diffused in air. Mechanical vapors
blended with fog: wires twisted and turned around clusters of bells
hanging from telegraph poles that uniformly followed each other.

★★★

Through red fractured walls, eaten by the fog, long streets open
silently. The vicious breathing darkens buildings, drapes the tops of the
towers and the long quiet streets, deserted as if after a robbery. The
figures of girls, all small, all dark, wrapped in elaborately knitted
scarves, pass, skipping through the streets, leaving them even emptier.
And in the nightmare of this fog, in that graveyard, they suddenly
seemed to me like countless tiny creatures, all alike, bouncing and
black, carrying their malicious conceit in a long insidious lethargy.

★★★

Numerous female students under porticoes; you immediately see that
we are in a center of culture. Casting occasional glances with Ophelic
innocence, three by three, whispering. A parade of pallid and fetching
modern graces formed under the colonnades: my classmates on their
way to a lecture! Not for them the forced D'Annuzian smiles quiver-
ing in the back of the throat, like a literary woman, more scarce and
severe is their smile, resolute and emaciated: prognosis withdrawn, like
a scientific woman.

★★★

(Caffe) The Russian woman passed by. The wound of her lips was burning on her pale face. She came and left, taking the flower and the wound of her lips: the cadence of her footsteps very elegant, but very self-aware. The snow kept falling and melting in the filth of the street, indifferently. The seamstress chatting with the lawyer, both laugh. Cloaked cabmen peeking out of their raised collars, like startled beasts. It's all the same to me. Today everything monotonous gray and dirty resurfaced in the city. Everything melts like snow in this swamp: and somewhere deep in my heart I feel the sweetness in the disintegration of all that which made us suffer. And even sweeter the snow will soon inevitably spread in white sheets, and we can rest again in our white dreams.

There is a mirror in front of me; the clock strikes: the light from the porticoes reaches me through the window drapes. I pick up the pen: I write: what, I don't know: I have blood on my fingers: I write: "the lover in the penumbra scratches at his lover's face to rip out his dream ... etc."

(Again on the street) Acute sadness. My old schoolmate stops me, back then he excelled in the literary arts, now he is a one-eyed, decrepit professor: he tempts me, confides in me with an increasingly dirty smile. He concludes: why don't you try to send something to the *Amore Illustrato.*

(Street). Here, under the porticoes, like the buzzing of an airplaine, an inevitable swarm of intellectual ladies who laugh and cackle, show-ing teeth in pursuit of, it seems, every enemy of science and culture, in order to tear them to pieces at the foot of the lecturn. It's time! I drag myself through the puddles in the middle of the street. Now the illustrious jackass will climb into the pulpit, carrying on his back the entire black catalog of scientific knowledge..................................
....
At the door of my house I turn around and see the typical enormous mustachioed policeman...
....
Ah! These rules of the venerable past! Ah! How many villains!

***

  (Night) In front of the fire, the mirror. In the bottomless phantas-
magoria of the mirror, naked bodies rotate silently: bodies prostrate
and engulfed in flame, ravenous and silent, and then as if outside of
time, the bodies: white, stupefied, listless in dead fires: white, from my
depleted spirit silent Eve disintegrates, and I wake up.

  I wander under the nightmare of the porticoes. A drop of bloodied
light, later a shadow, later, again, a drop of bloodied light, the sweet-
ness of the entombed. I disappear into an alley but from under a lamp
post a shadow disgorges a spectre, with tinted lips. Oh, Satan, you who
lay whores at the bottom of crossroads, oh, you who out of shadow
reveals Ophelia's vile corpse, oh, Satan, have mercy on my endless
suffering!

Takuboku Ishikawa

Building a New Metropolis
 — *translated by Peter Constantine*

Soon a worldwide war will come. Battle ships of the air will swarm
like phoenixes across the sky, the cities down below in ruins. A wide
expanse of war. And half of mankind will be nothing but bones. And
after that, misery, after that where will we build our new metropolis?
On the ruins of history? On deliberation or on love? No, no. On the
earth. Yes, on the earth. Up into an air that lacks the rules and distinc-
tions of matrimony. Beneath a limitless blue, blue sky.

[April 13, 1909]

Hagiwara Sakutarō

Inside the Panorama Hall
— *translated by Scott Mehl*

Look above you and there's a clear blue sky, which vaults downward to meet the horizon far away. All around you, vast plains stretch as far as the eye can see. Beyond, you can just make out the snow gleaming on mountaintops; clouds are hanging low on the horizon. Such a feeling of tranquility pervades the natural environment! And there, too distant to be made out clearly—are those clouds or mountains? In a reverie, I go wandering in pursuit of the farthest limit of pathos in this vast, vast world.

Hark—what is the source of the mournful tones I hear? A lugubrious music box, it must be, playing forgotten tunes, conjuring a vision of a forgotten century. Sad, melancholy, filled with sighs. O Marseille, Marseille, Marseille... From even further away, sounding like a far-off bugle, there comes the note of a contrabass, low but distinct. This ponderous note recounts a dream:

Like a dream, history fades into oblivion. The year is 1815; the place, the plain at Waterloo. That reed-filled river over there is the Maas. These houses here are a French village. Look in the history books: it is the 18th of June. The emperor of France, Napoleon I, and the allied Anglo-Prussian army have fought their final decisive battle here. And this is the French artillery position; the person on horseback atop the little hill is the great Napoleon Bonaparte. Standing beside him is Marshal Ney, nicknamed the Demon, the greatest commander under Napoleon. The massive force here in this field is the army led by the Duke of Wellington, an Englishman. Corpses of French soldiers lie in heaps here and there in the fields of wheat. The many gun carriages have been shot to pieces by pitiless enemy fire, and the vegetation gleams with fresh blood. O, Waterloo, dismal Waterloo. After his defeat the vaunted Napoleon I is taken prisoner and exiled on the remote island of Saint Helena. And look at this. These soldiers attempting a charge over here, the ones in three-cornered hats and wearing white cords crossing over their breasts, are Napoleon's Imperial Guard. Their flank is being shelled by a flying column of British infantry. And what looks like smoke over there on the far-off mountains is actually dust being raised by the Prussian reinforcements under Field Marshall Blücher. The year is 1815, the place is Waterloo, the French frontier. —O, O, like a dream, history fades into oblivion.

Pale smoke rises from the cannons all along the sunlit plain. Inside this dream of a peaceful sunlit day, in my imagination the whole sky thunders with cannon fire. There come the plaintive notes of what sounds like a subterranean music box, but where is it? O! old Panorama Hall! The Panorama Hall that I remember from my youth so long ago! It was pervaded with the air of past ages. At the end of a narrow corridor, in darkness under a blue tent, there hangs in the air, never extinguished, a solitary beam of light.

Georg Trakl

Winter Night
— *translated by John Hargraves*

Snow has fallen. After midnight, drunk with purple wine, you quit the
dark precinct of humans, the red flame of their hearth. Oh, the
darkness!

Black frost. The earth is hard, the air tastes of something bitter. Your
stars array themselves in evil patterns.

With stone-frozen steps you tramp along the railroad track, eyes
round with fear, like a soldier storming a black earthwork. Avanti!

Bitter snow…and moon!

A red wolf strangled by an angel. As you walk your legs clatter like
blue ice, a smile full of grief and arrogance has turned your gaze to
stone, and

Your brow turns pale in the ecstasy of frost; or it bends in silence over
the sleep of a guard sunk down in his wood hut.

Frost and smoke. A white shirt of stars burns the shoulders that wear
it, and God's vultures tear away at your metallic heart.

Oh, the hill of stones. Silently, and forgotten, the cold corpse melts
away in the silvery snow.

Sleep is black. The ear follows the long paths of the stars in the ice.
As you awoke, the village bells were ringing. Through the eastern gate
came the rosy day streaked with silver.

Pierre Reverdy

Squares
— *translated by Mary Ann Caws*

The shameful mask hid his teeth.
Another eye saw that they were false. Where
is it happening? And when? He is alone,
weeping, despite the pride bearing him
up, and he becomes ugly. Because it has
rained on the shoes, the other one said,
saliva on my shoes, I have become pale
and wicked. And he kissed the mask
which bit him as it sneered.

The profile, the same
profile as the great singer!
She wanted to have it, she
had it and also her
mammoth mouth without
her voice. But what she
most envied was the singer's
dress and never could she have it.

If you hear someone be-
hind you go Psst and a
taxi is passing at
the same time don't turn
around … it's for the taxi.

The hair cut, the head severed, the saber still remained between his teeth. The amateur executioner was weeping and his face was a mask. He had been imported from China and no longer knew how to be cruel.

I pass by being swallowed up, am swallowed up in a passing by. What an abyss! The head turning about me has disappeared. The birds were singing behind the window; they were singing off-key and were not dressed in real feathers.

The rum is excellent
The pipe is bitter and
the stars falling from
your hair fly off in
the fireplace.

From the binding of your lips from the binding of your shutters from the binding of our hands. Or perhaps easier. On the wooden balcony she kept watch in a dazzling nightgown.

After the first steps on his toes he had taken flight. The first clouds stop him. They are mirrors. And here again, where he discovered our world without flesh, he believed himself in heaven.

Liu Bannong

Rain
— *translated by Nick Admussen*

This is all in Xiaohui's words, I just took it down for her and linked it together, that's all.

Ma! Today I want to sleep — snuggle close to my mother and go to bed early. Listen! On the lawn behind you, there's not even a whisper; it's my friends, all snuggled up with their mothers and gone to bed early.

Listen! On the back lawn, there's not even a whisper; nothing but darkness like ink! Scary! Wild dogs and cats cry from far off, don't let them come! It's just the pitter-patter of rain, why is it still pattering out there?

Ma! I want to sleep! The rain that's not afraid of wild dogs or cats, it's still on the dark lawn, pitter-pattering. Why doesn't it go home? Why isn't it snuggled up with its mother, going to bed early?

Ma! Why are you laughing? You say it doesn't have a home? Yesterday when it wasn't raining, the lawn was all moonlight, where did it go? Does it have a mother? — didn't you say yesterday, the dark clouds in the sky, that's its mother?

Ma! I want to sleep! Close the window, don't let the rain in and make the bed wet. Give my rain jacket to the rain, don't let the rain get the rain's clothes wet.

Richard Aldington

Fatigues

The weariness of this dirt and labour, of this dirty melting sky!

For hours we have carried great bundles of hay from barge to truck, and from truck to train.

The weariness of this dirt and labour! But—look! Last June those heavy dried bales waved and glittered in the fields of England!

Cinque-foil, and clover, buttercups, fennel, thistle and rue—daisy and ragged robin, wild rose from the hedge, shepherd's purse a long sweet nodding stalks of grass!

Heart of me, heart of me, be not sick and faint though fingers and arms and head ache, you bear the gift of the glittering meadows of England. Here are bundles from Somerset, from Wales, from Hereford, Worcester, Gloucester—names we must love, scented with summer peace.

Handle them bravely, meadow-sweet, sorrel, lush-flag and arid knap-weed, flowers of marsh and cliff, handle them bravely!

Dear crushed flowers! And you, yet fragrant grasses, I stoop and kiss you furtively.

Dear gentle perished sisters, speak, whisper once more, tell me next June again you will dance and whisper in the wind.

Eugene Jolas

Monologue

I sleepwalk through the city and plunge into a golden smoke. What is my love for you, magical space and sinister time, when the dusk settles into marble and the owl is a categorical imperative? I left dream-staring puppets in a room, where the Ethiopian trembles at a blasphemy, and the sketch-book holds the contours of an atlas. The mother had a child in the dust and the lonely woman cried in a cafe. Then came a girl from out the autumnal solitude of her rooms, where she had stared at mirrors, and her silence was the dream of a midnight. Cool waters flowed under bridges and electric wires brought decay of flowers, tempests, portraits of nightmares, broken violins. Comrades walked tired into hurricanes. When the philosophies panted, and the symphonies ended in a shriek, stallions ground fire, and the bandits swilled brandy in an hallucinated den. The organ at the fair whimpered love-songs, but the funeral of the poor went past us with memories of loam. The trees became brass shining in sun. My waiting gulped bussed, tears, dust, drinks and sparrows.

Abraham Lincoln Gillespie

EXPATRACINATION1

(a) because in Europe I find MeaningScurry in their Organise-Self-Divert — hours loll here all simmer-rifeExpect-lush-stat, GET is less-necessary.

(b) because of the absence of Tight-blank faces here. (European Maturity seems of the in-touch-with-YouthPulse ripe sort[.]a)

(c) Liquor-Gamme abroad somewhat breatheier. (d) abroad, as if transplanted to an ideating DreamStanceIndef, the me-expatriate remenvisages America-theSpectacle, initsensing its cosmintegrality, critifocaspecting its Univeering probably for a first time. (local Econs are so intrude-mussuppy.)

the Spiritual Future of America is not to evolve till a present diabetes is admit > removed, t'wit: America's total lack of parent-sagacity to exprimply an especially-while-correctingthem goodwill toward, and to cull an early admiration from the children.

(The EffectLoss into Personality is enormous!! — contrast the majority of French Parents' Methattitude.)

THEN — the American Spirit will commence-sing as naivedirect-elimgoalpursue-clearly as its present FolkMelod "PopularSong," frequently as blare-Outr~Fruct-freely as its dynaSaxophoneyc. Neo-Polite-ObserveRigors will scourge off-away the become-cloyuseless of our present SklafManners — survive-a tiff with Russian Defeatind ivid-becomeCollectiMass output, our EconGrandees will have also residonned the surrealise raiment of skilledlaborer-integrality — the SportSense will have been furthalloted into a StreetPass-Calistheno (i.e. Fair, groove-compulsed into an inevitaBanter-Fair — we are a

Good Will-Collective — will assume social sensitude, a BodyClap-RazzCourtly deftjoice-skew-Apply-akin (somehow) to the finesse of France's Golden Period.

The Busybody-GoodWill will have insidAmericanized Europe (thru Dawesian EcoHighPressures, "Galette"-addvice, constant-rub-away of Europeans' giving in to the squarepeginsists of Fringlish-voicestressingl travellers and resiDents, spillover-manifest of America's Nth degree-PRODUCEMolochism, etc.) Semitised Russia will certainly psychYap doubly, its individuentsremainingscorn-evaded-Defeati speaking their present flapdoodleNonDigninhoIdliable'd rushout- heedless-O-Self! -stuff. (Russia's soon-enormous CollectiOutput will yet lag indef-behind America's shrewdingeniuity'd Get-Rich-Quick-Fellers!'d individ-catalysing Produce-Outvent.)

III. Communism, Surrealism, Anarchism — degrees of LyriProtestism — since Lyrism is based in Individualism the BureauLyrism of C. is an obvious paradox. — A.'s hysterlyr will always ultimately grudge-pend-ule-reactionate, stay the destroy-(to-begin-over)-hand (the subjectively A.'s applicable into a Recherche for the expression of the Consciousness betwixbeyond the Abstremities of Thought[)]l.s S., a French (psychanal-filtfree) Try has obviously essayed to continue "correctness," has but barely enlarged the GamutPossible of the Hithertooze-"Inadmissibie" — enlargers Braque, Ernst, Michonze, 4 obviously their Self; the rest, GoodManner'd Dada? — S. lacked gutsweat adherents collect-able to trek the toothsome of the Psych-RunningDown (In?) DreamStateProffClimbs-into-Reality which Andrt Breton skim-the-FreudSoup-touchly impicts. Possibly S. failed to posit a NeoAgonyProCreate.

IV. My work veer-expresses my relation to 20thCentury Reality, a relation I feel-think to be fillfuller than any hitherto CritiCommunic-Liable, i. e., mine, the necessity of lending consciousative LOGICAT-ING to the AromeClashBuildinnerising FORMTrends of Music's MelodSyntheBuildAlong, the gradaccrue of which (both delib and acciByProd) may-will tot-add sub-et-Supra integerCollects for furthing the Context'sI mputationise; at the same time possibuilding, in English — sole language evophonically free enuf to do so, — SensationForms rhapsintrest Composenuf to aesthConcomitate these neo-gather-imputes of Thought, i. e., the MarryMomelntentsity matings of hovexpecf Indeation & Vehicle-BecomePunct. My Article (transition 12)5 delineates the techBuild of this.

Paul Nougé

The ....
— *translated by M. Kasper*

Elvira is a ....., extremely .....

She's not like some ..... for whom .... is always too ...... and the ...
.... too ....

She knows that .... is necessary for ....

Not only her ... and her ...., but her neck, her arms, and her
shoulders are .... to .... every morning.

Often, she .... her ...... , her face, her whole body. She never uses
anything but .... : in summer, this .... ; in winter, she ......
herself and is quickly ......

She also enjoys a .....

Look how she's .... and .... : it's .... who gives her this ...
......

Follow the example of ....

Xu Zhimo

Poison
— *translated by Nick Admussen*

Today is not a day I'll sing, my mouth is twisted into a fierce, shameless smirk, and it's not a day I'll laugh or joke, my chest is pierced with an ice-bright blade;

believe me, my thoughts are malignant because the world is malignant, my spirit is dark because the sun's every radiance has been snuffed out, I speak with the voice of a graveyard owl because the human race has slain every vestige of harmony, I take the voice of an angry ghost raging against its enemies because all compassion has given way to enmity;

but believe me, there's truth in my words even though my words are like poison, truth is never ambiguous even though my words seem to speak with the tongue of a two-headed snake, the scorpion's tail, the centipede's venomed sting; it's simply that my heart is full of something more potent than poison, more vicious than curses, more furious than flame, more profoundly soft-hearted and pitying and compassionate than death, so what I say is toxic, is cursing, is searing, is empty;

believe me, all our measures have been sealed inside a mausoleum of coral stone, the aroma of the richest sacrificial feast could not penetrate its tight-sealed strata: all standards are dead;

all that we believe in is like a kite wrecked in a tree's upper branches, we raise the snapped-off kitestring in our hands: all beliefs have rotted;

believe me, the immense shadow of suspicion: like a dark cloud, it has cast a pall upon all human relations: children no longer wail at the death of their mothers, brothers no longer walk hand in hand with their sisters, friends have become foes, guard dogs turn to bite their masters: yes, suspicion has obliterated all; those sobbing by the road-side, those standing in the middle of the street, those peering at your window, they are all desecrated virgins: in the deep pond all that's visible are the fetid remains of the bright lotus blossom;

flowing down humanism's filthy mountain stream, as if floating, five mutilated corpses, those of kindness, justice, propriety, wisdom and faith, flow towards the boundless waves of time;

this ocean is not a peaceful ocean, billowing waves churn wildly, and atop each white cap desire and brutishness are clearly written;

everywhere are acts of adultery: greed pins and paws at righteous-ness, jealousy forces itself on sympathy, cowardice toys lewdly with bravery, lust bullies love, violence violates compassion, darkness tramples the light;

listen, oh listen, this perverse clamor, this din of brutality,

wolves and tigers stalk the bustling markets, thieves lie in the beds of your wives, there is evil in the depths of your souls....

Harry Crosby

from *Illustrations of Madness*

My heart is a madhouse for the twin lunatics of her eyes.

★

I rejoice in that dangerous automatic liberty which deprives man of the volition which constitutes him a being responsible for his actions.

★

I have heard for days and nights on end the reverberation crashing in my head of all the skyscrapers and buildings of the world, the reverberation of the crashing of ships in the fog at sea, the reverberation of the crashing of iron thoughts on the cold floor of the brain.

★

There is in me the infernal fury of the Sun by means of which I practice atrocities on the philistines. The operation of my fury is instantaneous and I abandon them to the malignity of my scorn and ridicule.

from *Dreams*

I.

the dream of the glass princess is a cool moonlight of glass wings each
wing a beat of the heart to greet the glass princess she is no bigger
than a thimble as she tiptoes daintily down the tall glass corridor of
my soul tinkle by tinkle tinkle until I feel I shall go mad with sus-
pense but just as she is opening her mouth to speak there is a shatter-
ing of glass and I awake to find I have knocked over the pitcher of ice
water that in summer always stands like a cold sentinel on the red
table by the bed.

II.

red funnels are vomiting tall smoke plumes gold and onyx and dia-
mond and emerald into four high round circles which solidify before
they collide together with the impact of billiard balls that soon are
caromed by a thin cue of wind into the deep pockets of sleep

Marcel Lecomte

Despair
   — translated by Michel Delville

In his delirium his ravings have been dreadful: he goes in all direc-
tions, running around the house, ramming into rooms over and over
again. It is as if the house was a place continually shaken by some
earthquake threatening to destroy it bit by bit, when it is not
possessed by fire, where lightning has fallen ...

Fall.

Ether

— *translated by Michel Delville*

The sky, a pale balloon on the sunny window of the antique dealer. This bedroom with washed out porcelain, where dreams are floating amongst monotonous sofas, encloses light sculpted in depth.

The musician's virgin eye meets the flowers of the wall, herbal blossom of the night.

Laura Riding

Mademoiselle Comet

We, then, having complete power, removed all the amusements that did not amuse us. We were then at least not hopelessly not amused. We inculcated in ourselves an amusability not qualified by standards developed from amusements that failed to amuse. Our standards, that is, were impossibly high.

And yet we were not hopeless. We were ascetically humorous, in fact. And so when Mademoiselle Comet came among us we were somewhat at a loss. For Mademoiselle Comet was a really professional entertainer. She came from where she came to make us look.

But Mademoiselle Comet was different. We could not help looking. But she more than amused. She was a perfect oddity. The fact that she was entertaining had no psychological connection with the fact that we were watching her. She was a creature of pure pleasure. She was a phenomenon; whose humorous slant did not sympathetically attack us; being a slant of independence not comedy. Her long bright hair was dead. She could not be loved.

Therefore Mademoiselle Comet became our entertainment. And she more than amused; we loved her. Having complete power, we placed her in a leading position, where we could observe her better. We were not amused. We were ascetically humorous. Thus we aged properly. We did not, like mirth-stricken children, die. Rather, we could not remember that we had ever been alive. We too had long bright dead hair. Mademoiselle Comet performed, we looked always a last time. We too performed, became really professional entertainers. Our ascetically humorous slant became more and more a slant of independence, less and less a slant of rejected comedy. With Mademoiselle Comet we became a troupe, creatures of pure pleasure, more than amused, more than amusing, looker-entertainers, Mademoiselle Comet's train of cold light. We were the phenomenal word *fun*, Mademoiselle Comet leading. Fun was our visible property. We appeared, a comet and its tail, with deadly powerfulness to ourselves. We collided.

We swallowed and were swallowed, more than amused. Mademoiselle, because of the position we had put her in with our complete power, alone survived. Her long bright dead hair covered her. Our long bright dead hair covered us. Her long bright dead hair alone survived; universe of pure pleasure, never tangled, never combed. She could not be loved. We loved her. Our long bright dead alone survived. We alone survived, having complete power. Our standards, that is, were impossibly high; and brilliant Mademoiselle Comet, a professional entertainer, satisfied them. Our standards alone survived, being impossibly high.

Kay Boyle

Summer

1

Flying curved to the wind shear-waters turn their bodies in the wave.
Sea hisses under the weed-hair, ice-armored foam plucked to vermil-
lion bubbles by the beak of the wind. Rocks crouch under the gold
hill where cypresses groove darkly like a negro lying down in wheat.

2

I press through the enclosing darkness to the window; Sky is torn
sharp as steel on the yucca horns, clouds pierced tight as whorls on
the yucca horns, plaques of firm flame-black on black embracing
darkness that curve up to sleek and handsome yucca horns.
Hysteria of the tress is palpable through the closed window and the
wall. The dry tongue of my sheet turns me slowly, tentatively.

3

Wind, tendinous, drifting dark and subtle in the channel, indolent,
with one arm stroking the shore. Reeds follow the movement, flow-
ing to light, following the mystery of muscles liberated under flesh.

Wind, fingering in the rain and the melon-flowers ... the black-
horned fungus growing under rye.

4

August crops wrinkled with young cabbages deplanted and wilting in
the new soil. Weight of the deflated flesh, the white-corded bellies,
topples the spindle-stems. Blood, still as a snail's track, bulges the blue
veins. There is an obscene chastity in the white potted skin. The white
peak of the leaf presses the dark soil, rearing the white body upward.

Fillìa

from *Mechanical Sensuality*
   — *translated by Jake Syersak*

adding machine

   anonymous mechanistic aid to an ever-multiplying useless cranial complexity

★

telephone

the ear dilutes itself via the auditory apparatus become the sensitive center of noise

it cannot help but hear why the outside world is breaking up against the small circular metallic plate

★

typewriter

    the hand becomes a rhythmic pulsation of movement a mechanism
rotated in the brain by the belts and pulleys of speed and persuasion

    it would be impossible to pursue a personal harmony   every-
thing is encased in the comprehensively-terse click of the small metal
buttons

★

typography

the sensible precision of the brain is translated into multitudinous possibilities multiplied through the inexhaustible mechanics of the printing presses

it is the cold progressive geometry of the human annulment absorbing every slow and expressive faculty into one insurmountably swift and simultaneous valorization of strength

it would be useless to pit the speed of such mechanics against the corpse-force of a multiplication long past its prime

★

telegraph

    words are the brain's rhythmic internalizations whose sounds are understood yet remain unfathomable

    the exasperation of the usual lucidity   immobile
coldly imposed   relentless

    the death of auditory sense

★

Poetry

stripped-down   sequestered   windowless room

white walls

one glossy table   two stools   one cold electric bulb
in a walk-in closet glass and steel receptacles for chemicals flowing
with prismatic liquids

one gas flame

silence

on one side   against the white wall   an invisible projection
reel (VITALITY) unwinds its synthetic cinematography

the brain absorbs every last scene transforming them mechanistically
through the liquid-sensations of its distilleries

Attila József

The Dog
— *translated by John Bátki*

He was shaggy, sloppy, wet, his coat a yellow frame. From his sad
haunches slim with hunger and seedy with desire the cool night
breeze streamed a long way. He ran and begged. Crowded, sighing
churches lived in his eyes as he scavenged for scraps and bread
crumbs.

I pitied him as if that poor dog had crawled out of myself.
I saw in him all that is shabby in this world.

We go to bed because we have to. Night puts us to bed and starvation
lulls us to sleep. But before falling asleep, while we lie like the city
silent under the chill vault of pure exhaustion, suddenly he comes out
of us, having laid low all day, that starved, muddy, ragged dog, to
scavenge for god-pieces.

Daniil Kharms

The Werld[8]
— *translated by Matvei Yankalevich*

I told myself that I see the world. But the whole world was not accessible to my gaze, and I saw only parts of the world. And everything that I saw I called parts of the world. And I examined the properties of these parts and, examining these properties, I wrought science. I understood that the parts have intelligent properties and that the same parts have unintelligent properties. I distinguished them and gave them names. And, depending on their properties, the parts of the world were intelligent or unintelligent.

And there were such parts of the world which could think. And these parts looked upon me and upon the other parts. And all these parts resembled one another, and I resembled them. And I spoke with these parts.

I said: parts thunder.

The parts said: a clump of time.

I said: I am also part of the three turns.

The parts answered: And we are little dots.

And suddenly I ceased seeing them and, soon after, the other parts as well. And I was frightened that the world would collapse.

But then I understood that I do not see the parts independently, but I see it all at once. At first I thought that it was NOTHING. But then I understood that this was the world and what I had seen before was NOT the world.

And I had always known what the world was, but what I had seen before I do not know even now.

And when the parts disappeared their intelligent properties ceased being intelligent, and their unintelligent properties ceased being unintelligent. And the whole world ceased to be intelligent and unintelligent.

But as soon as I understood that I saw the world, I ceased seeing it. I became frightened, thinking that the world had collapsed. But while I was thinking this, I realized that had the world collapsed then I would already not be thinking this. And I watched, looking for the world, but not finding it.

And soon after there wasn't anywhere to look.

Then I realized that since before there was somewhere to look—there had been a world around me. And now it's gone. There's only me.

And then I realized that I am the world.

But the world—is not me.

Although at the same time I am the world.

But the world's not me.

And I'm the world.

But the world's not me.

And I'm the world.

But the world's not me.

And I'm the world.

And after that I didn't think anything more.

[8] The title of this piece in Russian is *MYR*: a neologism formed from the combination of "*my*" ("we") and "*mir*" ("world"). I have approximated Kharms's neologism by combining the two English words.

Sleep Mocks a Man
— *translated by Matvei Yankalevich*

Markov took off his boots and, sighing, lay down on the couch. He wanted to sleep, but as soon as he closed his eyes, his desire to sleep instantly vanished. Markov would open his eyes and grope for a book.

But drowsiness would come over him again and, without reaching the book, Markov would lie back down and close his eyes again. But just as his eyes closed, sleep would drift away from him again, and his consciousness would become so clear that Markov could solve algebraic equations with two variables in his head.

For a long time Markov suffered in this way, not knowing what he should do: to sleep or to be wakeful? Finally, suffering all he could stand and growing to loathe himself and his room, Markov put on his coat and hat, and, with cane in hand, went out into the street. The fresh air calmed Markov. He felt at peace in his soul and a desire came upon him to return to his room.

Upon entering his room, he felt a pleasant exhaustion in his body and wanted to sleep. But as soon as he lay down on the couch and closed his eyes, his drowsiness instantly evaporated.

At wit's end, Markov sprung from the couch and without hat or coat rushed off in the direction of the Tavrichesky Garden.

Notes on the Poets

Richard Aldington was born in Portsmouth, in 1892, and died in Sury-en-Vaux, France in 1962. He met American poets Ezra Pound and Hilda Doolittle (H.D.), who had been previously engaged, and traveled with H.D. through Italy and France in 1913. Returning to London, they all lived in Churchwalk, Kensington, at number 6 (HD), number 8 (Aldington), and number 10 (Pound). Aldington and HD married in 1913, and it lasted until 1938. Aldington was an editor of the *Egoist,* author of the heavily censored *Death of a Hero* (1929), and he and H.D. were part of the imagist movement, inspired by Japanese verse forms, such as those advocated by T.E. Hulme, the important theorist of the movement. "Fatigues" is taken from the 1919 collection *Images of War.*

Born in 1876 in Camden, Ohio, **Sherwood Anderson** only became a full-time writer at the age of thirty six, after undergoing a nervous breakdown which led him to abandon a career as a businessman. Like Giovannitti's *Arrows in the Gale* (1914), Sherwood Anderson's prose hymns collected in *Mid-American Chants* (1918) testify to the development of a popular, "low modernist" tradition of the prose poem represented by a number of texts largely written out of the canon of American literature. Anderson's prose chants were soon to be followed by the picturesque idiosyncracies of his celebrated *Winesburg, Ohio* (1919) for which he achieved international fame. They owe as much to Whitman's declamatory style as to the prosodic techniques of the King James Bible. At the level of content, the book displays a grim vision of industrialized America marked by nostalgia for pre-industrial lore and the unmediated experience of rural Midwestern life. Anderson died in 1941 of an infection caught during a cruise to South America.

Charles Baudelaire's "petits poèmes en prose" were collected in *Paris Spleen,* a work begun in the mid-1850s and published in full in 1869. They are widely regarded as the originator of the prose poem form. Inspired as much by the poet's Symbolist aesthetics as by journalistic prose and the rhetoric of the *fait divers, Paris Spleen* sets itself the goal of reg-

istering the full spectrum of mental life and of reproducing the sinuos-
ities of human consciousness itself. In his Preface to the collection
Baudelaire memorably describes the prose poem as the ideal of "a poetic
prose, musical, without rhythm and without rhyme, supple enough and
rugged enough to adapt itself to the lyrical impulses of the soul, the un-
dulations of reverie, the jibes of conscience."

Louis Bertrand, who also wrote under the name of **Aloysius Ber-
trand**, was born in in 1807 in Ceva, which is now in Italy. His father
was in the military and Bertrand's family moved often until his father
retired to Dijon in 1815, where Bertrand mainly grew up. He attended
the Royal College of Dijon and moved to Paris in 1828 to be among
the Romantic poets, especially Sainte-Beuve. Bertrand wrote *Gaspard
de la nuit* in the early 1830s. His poor health forced him to return to
Dijon but he made it back to Paris in 1833 where he contracted tuber-
culosis, eventually succumbing to it in 1841. Throughout his life he had
numerous poems and articles published. *Gaspard de la nuit* was supposed
to have been published twice during Bertrand's lifetime, but was finally
published in 1842, the year after his death.

William Blake (b. 1757) was an English poet, painter and printmaker
born in London, where he died in 1827, on the eve of his 45th anniver-
sary. Blake was never wealthy and is said to have spent his last shillings
on a pencil to continue drawing his last series of illustrations for Dante's
Inferno. A mystic Christian raised in a family of English Dissenters, he
was convinced that spiritual experienced must come through personal
revelation and remained distrustful of all forms of organized religion.
Blake's visionary work (he had his first religious visions are the age of
four) was considered zany and insane by most of his contemporaries.
He has since then fascinated several generations of artists as diverse as
Aldous Huxley, C.S. Lewis, Georges Bataille, Allen Ginsberg, J. G. Ballard,
David Foster Wallace, and American rock band, The Doors. "A Mem-
orable Fancy" was taken from the 1790 collection *The Marriage of Heaven
and Hell,* a book of words and hand-painted images, whose plates were
colored by his wife Catherine.

Kay Boyle. Born in St. Paul, Minnesota, in 1902 died in Mill Valley, California, in 1992. Poet, novelist, and short story writer, she was also the author with Robert McAlmon of *Being Geniuses Together 1920–1930* (1968), an immensely informative work about the American writers in Paris in that period. Her many novels range from *Plagued by the Nightingale* (1931) through 1936, with *Death of a Man,* about the increasing threat of Nazism, to *Winter Night* of 1993. She married a French exchange student, Richard Brault, then lived with Ernest Walsh, until 1926, and after his death, lived with Laurence Vail from 1929, then married him in 1932, and after their divorce in 1943 married Baron Joseph von Franckenstein, and returned to the United States, where she was active in the NAACP and in Amnesty International. She was accused by McCarthy, lost her post as foreign correspondent for the *New Yorker,* and was finally cleared in 1957. She remained politically active, taught, joined writing colonies, and died in a retirement home in Mill Valley.

Dino Campana was born in 1885 in Marradi, a town near the border of Tuscany and Emiglia-Romagna. Often called an Italian poète maudit, Campana was a one-of-a-kind wanderer; outside of any kind of group, literary or social. Marginal to his core, he suffered from neurosis that propelled his body and mind towards incessant movement, rendering his aspirations intermittent and erratic. Frequent sojourns in mental institutions, unsuccessful attempts at academic scholarship, and extensive travel, including his voyage to Argentina and subsequent return to Italy, as a stowaway, by way of Odessa, disrupted his life. The fate of his only published work, a book of poems, *Canti Orfici,* was as tragic as was his life—the manuscript was overlooked then lost by Lacerba magazine's associate, Ardengo Soffici. A year later, the despondent poet rewrote these poems from memory and self-published in a local print shop. The poems, deeply introspective renderings of the poet's physical journey through Bologna, Genova, Argentina, and back, also contain references to his mystical searches for the time outside of space-time continuum. In 1918, following tumultuous and ultimately failed, love affair with the author Sibilla Aleramo, Campana was once again admitted to a psychiatric hospital in Scandicci, Florence, where he remained until his death in 1932.

Born in Villeneuve-sur-Fère in 1868, died in Paris, 1955, **Paul Claudel** was a celebrated playwright, diplomat, and essayist, author of *Connaissance de l'Est* (1900), *Cinq Grandes Odes* (1907) *L'Annonce faite à Marie* (1910), *La Jeune fille Violaine* (1926), and *Le Soulier de Satin* (1931). Converted at 18, hearing Vespers in the cathedral of Notre-Dame, he remained fervently religious; the "verset claudelien," named after his lengthy free verse, is modeled on the Psalms of the Vulgate, and is comparable to the verse of Walt Whitman. The lyric play *Partage de midi* (1906) takes its intensity from his love affair with a married woman, resulting in a child then adopted by Claudel and his wife; he committed his sister Camille to a psychiatric institution. We might well listen to the poet: "Qu'il ne reste plus rien de moi que la voix seule" ("Let nothing remain of me except my voice").

Samuel Taylor Coleridge was born in 1772 in Ottery St Mary, Devon, and died of a heart attack in Highgate, Middlesex. The son of a clergyman, he became one of the founders of the Romantic movement in England. With his friend William Wordsworth he published the *Lyrical Ballads* (1798), whose Preface has remained the most influential manifesto of the movement. Coleridge suffered from depression and ill-health for most of his life and developed an addiction to opium and laudanum. His "Vision in Dream", "Kubla Khan" (1816), was written under the influence of mind-altering drugs and is widely regarded as a precursor of psychedelic literature. Coleridge was also a distinguished literary critic and lecturer, known, amongst other things, for defending Shakespeare's *Hamlet* from its detractors, which included Voltaire and Dr Johnson. He had four children including the poet Hartley Coleridge and daughter Sara Coleridge, who became a writer and translator. A large selection of his notebooks were published in 1895 under the title *Anima Poetae* by Coleridge's grandson, Ernest Hartley Coleridge.

Sidonie-Gabrielle Colette was born in Saint-Sauveur-en-Puisay in Burgundy in 1873, and died in Paris in 1954, in her apartment in the Palais-Royal, having been a celebrated author, mime, actress, journalist, and photographer. She is perhaps best known for her 1944 novella *Gigi,* and *La Vagabonde* (1910), an inspiration for independent young women.

Married to Henry Gauthier-Villars ("Willy"), who published her first four Claudine stories under his name, she starred in music halls, sometimes with her lover Mathilde de Morny, the Marquise de Belbeuf ("missy"). She then married Henry de Jouvenel, and her novel *Chéri,* about an older woman and younger man mirrors her affair with her 16 year old stepson, as do some of her later novels. Finally, she married Maurice de Goudeket, and, unable to have a religious funeral because of her divorces, she was the first French woman of letters to be given a state funeral.

Harry Crosby was born in Boston in 1898, into a wealthy banking family. He is perhaps best-known as the co-founder, with his wife Polly (aka Caresse), of Black Sun Press, which published the early works of many young modernist writers including Ernest Hemingway, Hart Crane, D. H. Lawrence and Archibald MacLeish. His convulsed, strongly eroticized prose poetry was influenced as much by the French Symbolists as by T.S. Eliot, whom he admired. His work displays a strong oratorical strain, as well as a tendency to dwell on apocalyptic visions and various psychopathological states. His favored genres were the vision and the dreamscape, a preference he shared with other writers published in *transition* in the 1920s and 1930s such as Edouard Roditi, Charles Henri Ford, Marius Lyle (a pseudo for Mrs Waring Smyth) and Eugene Jolas. Crosby, who was fond of quoting Nietzsche's dictum that it is important "to die at the right time," died in New York City on December 10, 1929 in an apparent suicide pact with one of his lovers.

Rubén Darío, pseudonym of Félix Rubén García Sarmiento (born January 18, 1867, in Metapa, and died February 6, 1916, in León), was a Nicaraguan poet, journalist, and diplomat. He led the Latin American literary movement known as Modernismo, a reaction against literary naturalism that was informed by the European currents of Romanticism, Symbolism, and Parnassianism. Through his experiments with rhythm, meter, and sensuous imagery, and his use, in *Prosas profanas y otros poemas* (1896), of religious terms to express profane meanings, he revivified Spanish on both sides of the Atlantic. He left Nicaragua in 1886, beginning the travels that continued throughout his life.

Ernest Dowson was a poet, translator and fiction writer born in London in 1867. He was one of the main representatives of the British prose poem in the final years of the nineteenth century. His approach to poetic prose, like Oscar Wilde's, was inspired by the aesthetics of French Symbolism and favored the genres of the parable and the fairy tale. "Absinthia Taetra" is taken from *Decorations in Verse and Prose,* whose very title betrays its Decadentist undertones. Downson died in poverty and obscurity in 1900, at the age of thirty two, a few months before Wilde's final demise. On hearing of his death, Wilde wrote this: "Poor wounded wonderful fellow that he was, a tragic reproduction of all tragic poetry, like a symbol, or a scene. I hope bay leaves will be laid on his tomb and rue and myrtle too for he knew what love was."

Edward John Moreton Drax Plunkett (Lord Dunsany), 18th Baron of Dunsany. Born in London in 1878; died in Dublin in 1957. Lord Dunsany was an Irish fiction writer and playwright best known for his foundational role in the development the genre that came to be known as fantasy. H.P. Lovecraft, Robert E. Howard, Clark Ashton Smith, J.R.R. Tolkien, Fritz Leiber, Jack Vance and Michael Moorcock all recognized his significant influence on their respective works. "The Giant Poppy" (1915) is one of many tales of Fairyland, one which prefigures the dream-like atmospheres of his acclaimed 1924 novel *The King of Elfland's Daughter.* Dunsany's wonderous tales were praised by W. B. Yeats, who wrote that Dunsany "had transfigured with beauty the common sights of the world".

Frans Erens was born in 1857 in Limburg, a cradle of both medieval Dutch and German literature, which was not definitively made part of the Netherlands until a decade later. He spoke German, a local Germanic dialect and, thanks to his schooling, French. He studied law in Leiden from 1876, and moved to Paris for three years in 1880 to finish his studies. So Dutch, in a way, was a foreign language to him until adulthood. In Paris he was strongly influenced by Baudelaire's prose poems as well as by Rimbaud. His collection *Dansen en Rhytmen* (1893) explores this genre. Some texts explore contemporary urban life, others, like the text chosen, explore the role of rhythm and pulse. This prose poem *Golden Song* is intensely musical and impressionistic, with new verbal coinages also found in the "Tachtigers" movement of Dutch poetry.

Fillìa (1904–1935) was the pseudonym of the visual artist and writer Luigi Còlombo, a key organizer and theorist of the second wave of Italian Futurism. Fillìa was a prolific artist, authoring numerous paintings, novels, plays and contributing to a number of other projects, including cookbooks, manifestos, and various essays on architecture, design, and politics. Works of poetry published during his lifetime include *1+1 +1=1. Dinamite. Poesie Proletarie. Rosso + Nero* and *Lussuria radioelettrica*. He also contributed the 40 poems that comprise *Sensualità Meccanica* to the second major Futurist anthology *I nuovi poeti futuristi*.

Judith Gautier was born in Paris in 1845, and died in St. Enogat, Brittany, 1917. A French poet, novelist, and translator from Chinese and Japanese, she also wrote tales based on their histories. The daughter of the writer, Théophile Gautier, she married the poet Catulle Mendès, then separated from him, was the object of Victor Hugo's devotion, had an affair with Wagner in 1896 — for whom she would procure fabrics of his choice for his apparel and his decorations and staged his *Parsifal* with marionettes — and wrote about it in *Le Collier de mes jours* (1904), her memoirs. With Pierre Loti, she wrote a play called *La Fille du ciel* (Daughter of Heaven) Late in her life, she became the lover of Suzanne Meyer-Zundel, thirty-seven years younger, who had herself buried in Judith's grave in St. Enogat.

A maverick even among Modernist waters, **Abraham Lincoln Gillespie** was born in Philadelphia in 1885, then moved to France, where he led a bohemian life and met the likes of James Joyce, Georges Antheil, and Gertrude Stein, before returning to the United States in the early 1930s. Some of his eccentric poetic prose essays, bearing such titles as "Music Starts a Geometry" and "Textighter Eye-Ploy or Hothouse Bromidick?", were published in the 1920s and early 1930s in Maria and Eugene Jolas's little review *transition*, which also serialized sections from Joyce's *Work in Progress* (which later developed into *Fin-*

negans Wake). Kay Boyle and Robert McAlmon's memoir of the Paris expatriate crowd, *Being Geniuses Together,* pictures Gillespie as "a distorted caricature of Joyce" (he had been permanently disfigured at the age of twenty five owing to a car accident). Gillespie's work espoused the "Revolution of the Word" propounded by the Jolas and brought syntactic revolution to the history of the prose poetry.

Italian-American poet and social activist **Arturo Giovannitti** (1884 –1959) used prose poetry as an instrument of poetic expression of his socialist convictions. "The Walker," one of the most powerful poems of his *Arrows in the Gale* (1914), is a powerful synthesis of personal feeling and political commitment. The poem was inspired by Giovannitti's own time in prison awaiting trial for leading the famous Lawrence, Massachussetts strike of textile workers in 1912, after which he was framed on account of being accomplice to the death of a striker who was killed by the police. Singular missing element in the history of the American prose poem, Giovannitti's long-forgotten collection was made available again by Gian Lombardo's Quale Press in 2004.

Born at the Chateau le Cayla in the countryside near Toulouse in 1810, **Maurice de Guérin**'s writing was heavily influenced by nature. He was the younger brother of Eugénie, a writer noted for her journals and letters, who was a major influence and confidante. Maurice was raised a strict Catholic, and educated at a seminary in Toulouse. He studied at the College Stanislaus de Paris, where he met the novelist Jules Barbey d'Aurevilly. When he graduated in 1831 he lived in Brittany in a radical Christian society founded by de Lamennais. Two years later the society disbanded and de Guérin broke with Catholicism and moved to Paris. He fell ill and in 1839 died of tuberculosis at Le Cayla. Unpublished during his lifetime, George Sand published his prose poem *The Centaur* — the work he is most known for — and one of his poems in the *Revue des Deux Mondes.*

By the time of her death of leukemia at the age of 35 in 1913, the writer and artist, **Elena Guro**, a key figure in the early Russian avant-garde, had written three hybrid collections of prose, poetry and plays accompanied by her own drawings — *Hurdy-Gurdy, Autumn Dream,* and *Baby Camels of the Sky* (published posthumously)—as well as much uncollected work. Her writing was anthologized in several Fururist books and she belonged to the Union of Youth and the Cubo-Futurist group in Petersburg, where her and her husband Mikhail Matiushin's home (now a museum) served as a primary meeting place for artists and writers, including Malevich and Mayakovsky. Now known only in narrow circles, Guro's influence can be felt in the work of Khlebnikov, Tsvetaeva, and many others with whom she crossed paths.

Hagiwara Sakutarō (1886–1942) published his first poetry collection, *Tsuki ni hoeru* (Howling at the Moon), in 1917. This collection established at a stroke the viability of a more modern style in Japanese lyric poetry— one that did not rely on the tropes of the haiku and the tanka but instead seemed more of a piece with the prose style used in contemporary fiction. Hagiwara's subsequent poetry collections include *Aoneko* (The Blue Cat, 1923) and *Hyōtō* (The Iceland, 1934), the latter of which constituted a "retreat," as Hagiwara put it, to a more classicizing style, despite the evident modernity of the subject matter: alienation and mental distress. His prose works include books of aphorisms, prose poems, and critical writings: the monumental *Shi no genri* (Principles of Poetry, 1928) is a searching examination of the axioms of literary criticism.

Johann Christian Friedrich Hölderlin. Poet and philosopher (1770 born in Lauffen am Neckar — died 1843 in Tübingen 1843), Hölderlin was famous in German Romanticism and in German Idealism, associated with both Hegel and Schelling. Subject all his life to mental illness, and deemed incurable in 1806, he was lodged with a carpenter, Ernst Zimmer, for his last 36 years. Known for his novel *Hyperion,* he merged in his poetry Christian and Hellenic themes, and is known for his fragmentary writings, which greatly influenced Paul Celan and other recent poets. His renderings of Sophocles were saluted by Walter Benjamin as a new model for poetic translation. "In Lovely Blue" originally appeared in prose form in Wilhelm Waiblinger's 1823 novel *Phaeton.* Waiblinger was a university student who visited the poet regularly in the early 1820s and claimed to have taken it down as dictation.

Joris-Karl Huysmans was born in Paris in 1848, where he died of cancer in 1907. His oeuvre spans a multitude of styles and registers from his early naturalist fiction to his Decadent period — marked by his celebrated *A Rebours* (1884) — and on to the late religious novels (*L'Oblat,* 1903). Des Esseintes, the protagonist of *A Rebours,* defines the prose poem as "the concrete pith, the osmazome of literature, the essential oil of art." Whereas De Esseintes defines the genre as a concentrated version of the novel, Huysmans himself began his career as a prose poet (*Le Drageoir aux épices,* 1874). The *Drageoir* was followed by *Croquis Parisiens* in 1880. While Huysmans's prose poems are clearly marked by the legacies of Charles Baudelaire ("Camaïeu rouge" is a case in point) and Aloysius Bertrand (like his predecessor, *Gaspard de la nuit,* the *Drageoir* amply references Rembrandt), they also evidence the author's growing fascination with Zola's naturalist models and principles.

Takuboku Ishikawa (1886–1912) was a master of traditional Japanese Tanka poetry and a leading figure of Japanese naturalism. His poetry was remarkable in that it strictly followed the traditional thirty-one syllables with which the Tanka had been composed since before the fifth century CE, but was written in a striking blend of classical and contemporary language, his themes centering on his troubled inner life as a man struggling to survive the impersonal urban sprawl of Tokyo. Takuboku kept a diary in which he recorded his daily life and thoughts with disarming honesty. (He wrote it in Roman letters so that his wife would not be able to read it.) The prose poem in this anthology is from his diary.

A French poet, painter, writer, born in Quimper in 1876, **Max Jacob** was deeply connected to Brittany. After being seized from his monastic retreat in St. Benoît-sur-Loire by the Nazis, he died in the Drancy internment camp in 1944. Close always to Picasso, to whom he taught French, and Apollinaire (see Picasso's celebration of their threesome, *Les Trois Musiciens*), he worked in the orbit of Cubism and much more, leaving an immense impression on poets all over the world. A Jewish homosexual, he was famously converted by a vision of Christ in 1909, and his writings mirror the complications of his life. They include the novel *Saint Matorel* (1911), *Le laboratoire central* (1921), in *vers libres,* and *La défense de*

Tartuffe (1919), arguing with religious and personal attitudes, while he is perhaps best known to the poetic world for his *Cornet à Dés* (1917), that *Dice Cup* that clearly situates him between Symbolism and Surrealism.

John George Eugène Jolas was born in 1894 in Union Hill, New Jersey, and died 1952 in Forbach, Lorraine. A writer, translator, literary critic and, with his wife Maria McDonald and Eliot Paul, founded the international literary magazine *transition,* publishing Beckett, Gertrude Stein, and other avant-garde writers. He and Maria supported James Joyce and his Work in Progress, which turned out to be *Finnegans Wake.* He was a reporter for the European edition of the *Chicago Tribune in Paris*, then took over the literary page, and wrote a weekly column, "Rambles through Literary Paris." His *Revolution of the Word Manifesto* states the abolition of time and that the plain reader should "be damned." As a translator, he is best known for his rendering of *Berlin Alexanderplatz* into English in 1931.

James Joyce. Born in Rathgar, Ireland, in 1882; died in Zürich in 1941. In 1902, Joyce, then a twenty-year-old undergraduate, boasted to William Butler Yeats that he had abandoned metrical form and created "a form so fluent that it would respond to the motions of the spirit". Joyce's "epiphanies" used poetic prose as a vehicle for approaching the capricious flow of consciousness famously described by Baudelaire in his Preface to *Paris Spleen.* Some of them were later recycled into the novels which took him to the pinnacle of experimental modernism. The posthumously published *Giacomo Joyce* is a collection of lyrical prose fragments all related to a single subject: Joyce's infatuation with one of his girl students in Trieste, whom the author's biographer, Richard Ellmann, identifies as Amalia Popper, the daughter of a Triestine Jewish businessman. The explicitly autobiographical character of the poem and the embarrassing nature of the subject prevented Joyce from publishing the work in its original form.

Attila József (1905–1935) was the son of a soap maker and a laundry woman. He suffered from a lack of recognition throughout his life and one has to wait until the 1960s to see him recognized as one of the most important and influential representatives of Hungarian modernism. With the help of a few supporters of modernist literature, including Lajos Hatvany, he went to study at the University of Vienna (1925), then at Sorbonne (1926). While in Paris, he joined the Union Anarchiste-Communiste. In 1927 in returned to Hungary where he published in various left-wing periodicals. His poetry and essays attempt a synthesis of marxism and freudianism. His interest in psychoanalysis got him expelled of the Hungarian Communist Party in 1936. Jószef suffered from mental illness throughout his life. He was crushed by a train while crossing railway tracks near his sister's house in Balatonszárszó, where he was recovering from increasingly frequent bouts of depression and neurasthenia.

Franz Kafka was born in Prague in 1883 and died from tuberculosis in 1924 in a sanatorium near Vienna. Trained as a lawyer, Kafka spent much of his short life working as an insurance company clerk, writing fiction in his spare time. He is perhaps best known for his short story "The Metamorphosis", first published in 1915, in which he created a fictional world dominated by the uncanny, the meaningless, the dark burlesque and the absurd. The question of whether "Nachts" (At Night") should be regarded as a very short story or a parable or a prose poem matters less than the huge influence he has exerted on several generation of writers, some of them prose poets, marked by his peculiar brand of magic realism and his preoccupation with the metaphysical absurdity of human existence. In his short story "On Parables", one of his characters argues that "parables are only trying to say that the incomprehensible is incomprehensible."

Kanbara Ariake (1876–1952) has been called one of the principal poets of Japanese Symbolism. In the first decade of the twentieth century he published four collections of poetry, culminating in the *Ariake shū* (Ariake Anthology) of 1908. His metrical facility in modern Japanese lyric was and remains unmatched: he prolifically invented new meters and stanza forms, dramatically expanding the prosodic possibilities of the Japanese language. But the vogue for free verse, which began being written in Japanese in late 1907, caused a decisive turn away from metrically regular longer lyric in Japanese, and Ariake's work lost its readership. Ariake was the first to present versions of Baudelaire's French prose poems in Japanese and was among the first Japanese poets to compose *sanbunshi* (prose poems). Ariake spent the last four decades of his life far from the centers of literary activity and died in obscurity.

Daniil Kharms (1905–1942) was an early Soviet children's writer and co-founder of the avant-garde performance and poetry group, the OBERIU, or Union of Real Art. In 1931, along with other "*oberiuty*," he was swept up in arrests of "anti-Soviet children's writers." Upon his return from a brief exile from Leningrad, the political climate made it impossible for the OBERIU to perform, and by the late 1930s, it became difficult to publish his work for children. Kharms lived in debt and hunger for several years until his final arrest on suspicions of treason in the summer of 1941. He was locked up in a prison psychiatric ward and died of hunger during the Siege of Leningrad. His work was saved from his apartment by loyal friends and hidden until the 1960s, when his children's writing was republished to popular acclaim, and his manuscripts surfaced in *samizdat* and western publications.

Marcel Lecomte is a Belgian Surrealist poet born in Brussels in 1900. With Paul Nougé and Camille Goemans, he founded *Correspondance*, the first Belgian Surrealist "mail art magazine" in 1924, the same year as André Breton's first Surrealist Manifesto. Like Nougé, Lecomte remained suspicious of Breton's automatic writing and adopted a more restrained and melancholy style inspired by Henri de Régnier, whom he acknowledges as one of his earliest influences. Lecomte is also the author of many art chronicles on artists ranging from contemporary Surrealist painters to Vélasquez or Brueghel. He worked as a secondary school teacher for many years until he became attached to the Musées Royaux des Beaux-Arts de Belgique from 1960 to his death, in 1966. "Despair" and "Ether" are taken from his third book, *Applications,* published in in 1925, which also included illustrations by René Magritte, who portrayed Lecomte in his 1955 painting "Souvenir de Voyage III".

Liu Bannong (1891–1934) was a writer, translator, linguist, and teacher. Early in his career he published fiction, poetry, song lyrics and translations in the burgeoning commercial print culture of Shanghai; between 1916 and 1918, he transformed himself through the study and translation of poetics and poetry, and spent the rest of his life as a Beijing-based intellectual and professor of phonology. Although his poetry collections *The Earthen Pot* (瓦釜集) and *Flourishing the Whip* (扬鞭集) were influential, he rejected the title of "poet." He was likely the first person to translate the phrase *prose poetry* into Chinese; he also created the female third person pronoun ta (她).

Amy Lawrence Lowell. Born in Boston in 1874 and died there in 1925. She traveled extensively, and with the actress Ada Dwyer Russell, for whom she wrote many love poems, such as "Two Speak Together," went to England, where Lowell met Ezra Pound, who became a major influence and a major critic of her work. She is associated with imagism, to the point that her poems are sometimes called "Amygism". Lowell wrote in free verse, and dispensed with line breaks, calling her writing "polyphonic prose." She wrote on French literature, reworked some translations of Chinese poetry, and has to some extent been rediscovered by the women's movement.

Mina Gertrude Lowy (Mina Loy). Born in 1882 in London, died in 1966, in Aspen, Colorado. Poet, painter, playwright, essayist, she was half-Jewish through her father and half-Protestant through her mother. Raised in London, studied art in Munich, then in London, married the photographer Stephen Haweis in Paris in 1903, and changed her name to Loy. After her first child died suddenly, Mina and Haweis moved to Florence, where her daughter Joella was born in 1907, and a son, Giles in 1909, who was taken away by Haweis and died in 1912. After tumultuous affairs in 1914 with the Futurists Marinetti and Papini in Florence, she met in New York her one great love, Arthur Cravan, writer, boxer, and much else, and married him in 1918. After his mysterious disappearance, their daughter Fabienne was born in 1919. After a time in Paris, struggling as a designer, Mina returned to New York, and then to Aspen in 1953 to be with her daughters, leaving a mass of incompleted manuscripts. A lifelong practitioner of Christian Science, she became close friends with another Scientist, Joseph Cornell.

Lu Xun (1881–1936) is one of China's most influential writers. An early and powerful proponent of modern vernacular language, his short story collection *Call to Arms* reflected, and then came to epitomize, the early twentieth century Chinese movement to replace imperial traditions with modern, progressive language, culture, and values. As the revolutionary moment of his youth waned, he turned away from fiction and wrote *Weeds*, a collection that he said "to exaggerate a little bit, is prose poetry." Soon after, he would revolutionize a third genre, that of the daggerlike zawen (杂文) essay. Lu Xun has been read and idolized across the twentieth century: Mao Zedong called him a "modern sage" equal to Confucius; dissident and Nobel Laureate Liu Xiaobo said he is the Chinese people's "most necessary spiritual resource."

Stéphane Mallarmé (1842–1898), most influential for his verse poem "L'Après-midi d'un faune" and his experimental work "Un Coup de Dés", also wrote enigmatic but beautifully crafted sonnets, and a series of innovative prose poems. A friend of artists and musicians, his work, both creative and critical, offers a highly original aesthetic which was to exert considerable influence over later writers.

A member of a reform-minded generation of Japanese writers, **Masaoka Shiki** (1867–1902) made two signal contributions to Japanese literature: he reoriented haiku criticism, treating it as a creative activity of the greatest import; and through that very criticism, he fortified the bases of haiku composition. Even without Shiki's work, it is just possible that the haiku would have survived the many changes that took place in Japanese literature in the late nineteenth and early twentieth centuries; but with the work of Shiki and his followers, the haiku thrived. Shiki spent the last five years of his life invalided by the tuberculosis of which he would die; the diaries he composed while bedridden—among them *Bokujū itteki* (A Drop of Ink) and *Gyōga manroku* (Supine Miscellany)—include exceptionally fine passages of modern Japanese prose.

Mizuno Yōshū was born in 1883 in Tokyo but spent his youth in the city of Fukuoka, Kyūshū. When he succeeded in publishing a poem in 1900, he devoted all his energies to writing, returning to Tokyo to live a literary life. In Tokyo he joined literary coteries and began what would be lifelong friendships with the lyric poet Takamura Kōtarō and the tanka poet Kubota Utsubo. Mizuno came to be known for his *shōhinbun* (short prose pieces), of which he published his first collection in 1908. His later writings ranged from the folklore of the Tōno region in Japan, to spiritualism, to Japanese script reform. Influenced partly by Takamura and partly by the thought of Lev Tolstoy, Mizuno eventually distanced himself from modern urban culture, relocating his family to a small-holding outside Tokyo, where he lived for the last twenty-four years of his life. He died in 1947.

Paul Nougé was born in Brussels in 1895 (d. 1967). He was a founding member of both the Belgian Communist Party and the Belgian Surrealist Group. He worked as a biochemist and wrote on the side, but wasn't much published until late in life and posthumously. His notions on and diverse demonstrations of plagiarism as a literary strategy foreshadowed and influenced Situationist détournements. Nougé's poetry is alternately lyrical, scientific, dialectic, polemical, erotic, and analytical. Many of his writings are informed by his scientific background, and some have seen in the tacking dialectics of his prose poetry a prefiguration of the theory of complex systems. In one of his fragments, Nougé explains that "poetry offers the singular spectacle of analytical thought deploying itself, deploying itself against analysis". A man of many trades and talents, Nougé also wrote lyrics for the French singer Barbara.

Pierre Reverdy was born in Narbonne in the south of France in 1889 and died in Solesmes, near a Benedictine monastery in the northeast of France, in 1960. In Paris he was close friends with the Montmartre poets and painters, including the cubists Max Jacob, Guillaume Apollinaire, and Juan Gris. He founded the literary magazine *Nord-Sud* (1917–1918), named for the subway line from the north to the south of Paris. Among his volumes of poetry are *Poèmes en prose* (1915) illustrated by Juan Gris,

Les Ardoises du toit (1918), and *Le Chant des morts* (1948), this in collaboration with Picasso. Reverdy was a member of the Resistance during the Occupation.

Laura Riding. Born in New York City in 1901 and died in Sebastien, Florida in 1991. Through Allen Tate, she became associated with the Fugitives, met and married Louis R. Gottschalk, and after their divorce in 1925, she went to England, invited by Robert Graves and Nancy Nicholson his wife, moved in with them, attempted suicide, then invited the Irish poet Geoffrey Phibbs in 1929 to join their household, which he did, changed his mind, returned to his wife, then came back and ended up with Nancy. On April 27, 1929, Riding jumped out a fourth-floor window. Graves jumped after her but was unharmed, while she was gravely harmed. Much scandal ensued about them all. Then Riding and Graves lived in Majorca, visited by many artists and writers, left Majorca in 1936 at the outbreak of the Spanish Civil War, and after 1939, returned to New Hope, Pennsylvania. They separated and she married Schuyler B. Jackson, moving with him to Wabasso, Florida. *A Survey of Modernist Poetry* edited by Graves and Riding was the basis of Empson's *Seven Types of Ambiguity*.

To many contemporary readers **Rainer Maria Rilke** is best known for his posthumously published "Letters to a Young Poet," addressed to Austrian military officer and journalist Franz Xaver Kappus, and for the widely read and taught poem "The Panther", with which the *Dinggedicht* "The Lion Cage" shares a number of formal and thematic features. He was influenced by visual artists such as Cézanne and Rodin, with whom he became associated when he moved to Paris in 1902 and to whom he devoted a substantial essay. While his early, struggling years in France are documented in his semi-autobiographical novel *The Notebooks of Malte Laurids Brigge*, his *Duino Elegies* (1923) are marked by a metaphysical and visionary style often verging on the mystical. Rilke's influence on world literature is immense, as is his importance as a transitional figure from *fin-de-siècle* Decadentism to Modernism. Rilke died from leukemia in the Valmont Sanatorium in Switzerland in 1926.

Arthur Rimbaud (1854–1891) is among the rare poets whose legend threatens to overshadow the work. His escape to Paris at age seventeen to join a circle of cutting-edge poets, his scandalous and violent affair with Paul Verlaine, and his years as a trader and gun-runner in Africa are familiar even to many who have never read a word of his writing. But this should not obscure his crucial role in the evolution of modern poetry. Rimbaud's experiments — his insolent stances as much as his tonal innovations and explorations of the prose form as a poetic vehicle — have influenced figures as diverse as Paul Claudel, André Breton, and Patti Smith. The freewheeling attitudes he conveyed in works such as *Illuminations* and *A Season in Hell* foreshadow the brashness of the Sixties, and have much to say to young readers today. The "man with soles of wind," as Verlaine dubbed him, remains eternally elusive, eternally provocative.

Victor Segalen was born in Brest, Brittany in 1878. He was a poet, novelist, playwright, archeologist, art critic, linguist — and naval doctor. His literary output goes against the grain of turn-of-the century exoticism, which he derided as "palm trees and caravans; pith helmets; black skins and yellow suns," in his *Essai sur L'exotisme: An Aesthetics of Diversity* (1908). His travels in Tahiti and China, where he lived for several years, are the setting for several of his major works, the novels *Les Immémoriaux* (1907) about the decline of Maori civilization after contact with the West, *Le fils du ciel. Chronique des jours souverains*, recounting a powerful Chinese emperor's reign sapped by foreign invasion and political intrigue, and *René Leys*, set in Peking during the months leading up to the abdication of the Qing Dynasty in 1911, (posthumously published in 1922). With *Stèles* (1920), Segalen devised a new poetic form inspired by the hieratic inscriptions on the stone tablets he came upon in the Chinese landscape during archaeological expeditions. In 1919, Segalen was found dead in a forest near Brest.

William Sharp was born in Paisley, Scotland, in 1855 and died in Bronte, Sicily in 1905. He published a series of Gaelic romances, stories and prose poems under the pseudonym "Fiona Mcleod". Macleod became a prominent figure in the Celtic movement, and many believed that Yeats and Macleod were the same person. Whenever Sharp had to answer letters in her name, these were dictated to his sister, Mary Beatrice Sharp, whose handwriting became known as Fiona's. Sharp's secret was only revealed to his wife Elizabeth on his deathbed. In addition to his poetic work, Sharp wrote important literary essays, notably on Symbolist Belgian art, and biographies of Percy Bysshe Shelley, Robert Browning, Heinrich Heine and Maurice Maeterlinck.

Gertrude Stein was born 1874 in Pittsburgh, died 1946 in Paris. Essayist, poet, art collector, and host of a Parisian artist salon. She was raised in Oakland, California, educated at Radcliffe, where she studied under William James, and Johns Hopkins where she studied medicine. She moved to Paris in 1953, and, with her brother Leo, moved in avant-garde literary and artistic circles, and collected art by Picasso, Masson, Matisse, and others famous and less so. Her celebrated salon on the rue Fleurus she shared with her lifetime partner, Alice B. Toklas. Most famous works, among many others, include *Three Lives* (1909), *Tender Buttons* (1914), *The Making of Americans* (1925), *The Autobiography of Alice B. Toklas* (1933), and *Everybody's Autobiography* (1937). Stein exerted a powerful influence on literary and artistic modes and persons worldwide.

Georg Trakl. Born in Salzburg February 1887, died in Krakow, November 1914. Austrian expressionist, poet, writer, playwright, pharmacist and close to his sister Grete. Ludwig von Ficker, editor of journal *Der Brunner* helped him publish poems, and his *Gedichte* were brought out by Kurt Wolff in Leipzig, 1913. Ludwig Wittgenstein anonymously provided him a stipend. Medical officer in Austro-Hungarian Army, on Eastern Front. In 1914, he fought in the Battle of Grodek, and his best known poem bears that title. He suffered bouts of grave depression after helping wounded soldiers, and attempted suicide then, but was taken to a military hospital in Krakow, where he died shortly before Wittgenstein's arrival to see him. He was buried alongside Ficker in the municipal cemetery of Innsbruck-Mühlau. Many of his poems are set to music and dance.

Born in Oryol in western Russia in 1818, **Ivan Turgenev**, a pillar in Russian literature, spoke only French until he was nine years old. He learned Russian in secret, studying with one of the household's serfs. *A*

Sportsman's Sketches (1852), a breakthrough in Russian Realism, established Turgenev as a seminal stylist of Russian literature, second only perhaps to Vladimir Nabokov; his exquisite painterly representations of landscape remain unmatched. One of the most empathetic of the greatest 19th-century Russian writers, Turgenev was also exceptional in his apprehension of the social life in the coeval epoch—he brought the term "nihilism" into the mainstream of the Russian and the Western intellectual thought, first introducing it in his most successful novel *Fathers and Sons* (1862). He died in 1883 in Bougival, France, where he moved to pursue the love of his life, opera singer Pauline Viardot (1821–1910).

Renée Vivien, also Paule Riverdale (Pauline Mary Tarn). Born in London in 1877, lived in Paris, wrote in French, and died of self-starvation in Paris in 1907. Known for her various passionate poems in several volumes, and her famous relation between 1900 and 1905 with Natalie Barney — "L'Amazone," "La Très Blonde," her "Lorely" who welcomed the celebrated, artistic, lesbian, and beautiful and less so, in her Temple d'Amitié at 20 rue Jacob, and died at 96 in 1972. Vivien's dream of a lesbian colony in Mytilène (thus earning the name "Sappho 1900" and referred to by Nicola G. Albert, in her celebratory centenary volume Renée Vivien à rebours, as "Psappha loving Atthis" — imitating her lisp) inspired other women poets, as did her own complicated involvements with Violette Shillito, Eva Palmer, Kérimé Turkhan Pacha, la baronne Hélène de Zuylen, and her representation in Le Pur et l'Impur of Colette ("Missy"). Her *Brumes de Fjords/Fogs of Fjords* are her French translations of Norwegian poems, enlisting the haze of different atmospheres as her incessant travels, neurosthenia, and isolation, all clouded over any sure sense of her being, perhaps discoverable in her diary: *Ma Vie et mes idées.* She was converted to Catholicism on her deathbed. Her collection of Buddhas is found in the Musée Cernuschi in Paris.

Oscar Fingal O'Flahertie Wills Wilde was born in Dublin in 1854, and died in Paris in 1900. Playwright, poet, storyteller, and novelist. Having had a French nurse maid and a German govenness, he knew those languages, and his famous play *Salomé* (performed in 1902) is written in French. *The Picture of Dorian Gray* (1890) has a picture age instead of the hero, his play *The Importance of Being Earnest* (1895) is still performed, his fairy stories in *The Happy Prince* (1888) delight readers of all ages. Among his tutors at Oxford were Walter Pater and John Ruskin, associated with his "aestheticism," about which his writings are assembled in *Intentions* (1891). He was arrested for "gross indecency" with men, convicted and sent to jail from 1895–1897, where he wrote his letter *De Profundis* (published posthumously in 1905), and his last work, *The Ballad of Reading Gaol* (1898) a long poem about the imprisonment.

Adeline Virginia Woolf. Born in London in 1882, died near Lewes, Sussex, in 1941. The daughter of Lesley Stephen, the editor of the *Dictionary of National Biography,* and the beautiful Julia Jackson, she married Leonard Woolf, with whom she founded the Hogarth Press. She was a central character in the Bloomsbury group, along with Roger Fry, Maynard Keynes, Duncan Grant, and Lytton Strachey, and Clive Bell. Her novels include *Mrs. Dalloway* (1925), *A Room of One's Own* (1929), *To the Lighthouse* (1927), *Orlando* (1929), and *The Waves* (1931). She had a famous two-year affair with the writer Vita Sackville-West, with whom she remained close friends. Plagued by ill health and bouts of actual madness, she committed suicide by drowning in the river Ouse.

Xu Zhimo (1897–1931) is one of China's most famous modern poets, and the author of the collection *Zhimo's Poems.* A widely traveled, multilingual reader and translator, he helped build Chinese modern vernacular poetry in part by adapting and transforming English and French traditions from the sonnet to the prose poem to Symbolism and Romanticism. His poem "Farewell to Cambridge" is taught in all Chinese schools as an exemplar of modern poetry. He led a famously dramatic personal life, and is proven or rumored to have romantic connections to some of China's most distinguished intellectual women; he died in a plane crash at the age of 34.

Notes on the Translators

Nick Admussen is an associate professor of Chinese Literature and Culture at Cornell University. He is the author of the scholarly monograph *Recite and Refuse: Contemporary Chinese Prose Poetry,* the translator of Ya Shi's poetry collection *Floral Mutter*, and the author of two chapbooks of original prose poetry.

John Bátki is a writer, poet, translator and kilimologist born in Hungary, who moved to the United States in 1957, where he now lives and works. Batki has had his work featured in *The New Yorker*, taught at Harvard University, and has received several accolades for his work, including the O. Henry Award. He has translated book-length collections by Attila József, Ivan Mandy, and Gyula Krúdy.

Chris Campanioni was born in Manhattan in 1985. He is the author of six books, including *A and B and Also Nothing* (Otis Books | Seismicity Editions, 2020), a re-writing of Henry James's *The American* and Gertrude Stein's "Americans" which merges theory, fiction, and autobiography. His selected poetry was awarded an Academy of American Poets College Prize in 2013, his novel *Going Down* was named Best First Book at the 2014 International Latino Book Awards, and his hybrid text "This body's long (& I'm still loading)" was adapted as an official selection of the Canadian International Film Festival in 2017. Recent writing has appeared in *American Poetry Review, Poetry International, Ambit,* and *Nat. Brut,* and has been translated into Spanish and Portuguese. He edits *PANK* and lives in Brooklyn.

Mary Ann Caws is Distinguished Professor Emerita of Comparative Literature, English, and French at the Graduate School of CUNY. She is an *Officier of the Palmes académiques*, a *Chevalier dans l'ordre des Arts et des Lettres*, holds a DHL from Union College, is the recipient of Guggenheim, Rockefeller, and Getty fellowships, a fellow of the American Academy of Arts and Sciences, and the past president of the MLA and of the ACLA. She is the author of *The Eye in the Text, The Surrealist Look:*

an Erotics of Encounter, The Modern Art Cookbook, Blaise Pascal: Miracles and Reason, Creative Gatherings: Meeting Places of Modernism, a translator of Mallarmé, Char, des Forêts, Reverdy, Breton, Desnos, and the editor of HarperCollins World Literature, The Yale Anthology of Twentieth Century French Poetry, The Surrealist Painters and Poets, and Milk Bowl of Feathers: Essential Surrealist Writings.

Roger Célestin is Professor of French and Comparative Literature and chair of French and Francophone Studies at the University of Connect-icut. He has written on travel literature, detective fiction, film, and trans-lation, among other topics. He is the author of From Cannibals to Radicals. Figures and Limits of Exoticism, co-editor of Beyond French Feminisms: De-bates on Women, Politics, and Culture in France, 1980–2001 and co-author of Universalism in Crisis: France from 1851 to the Present. He is co-founder and editor of Contemporary French & Francophone Studies: SITES.

Peter Constantine is a literary translator and editor. His translations include Sophocles's Theban Trilogy, The Essential Writings of Machiavelli, and works by Gogol, Tolstoy, Dostoevsky, and Voltaire. He co-edited A Century of Greek Poetry: 1900–2000 and the anthology The Greek Poets: Homer to the Present (Norton). A Guggenheim Fellow, he was awarded the PEN Translation Prize for Six Early Stories by Thomas Mann; the Na-tional Translation Award for The Undiscovered Chekhov: Thirty-Eight New Stories; a Koret Jewish Book Award and a National Jewish Book Award citation for his translation of The Complete Works of Isaac Babel; the 2004/2005 Hellenic Association of Translators of Literature Prize for his translation of the modern Greek poet Stylianos Harkianakis's poetry book Mother; and the Helen and Kurt Wolff Translator's Prize for his translation of Benjamin Lebert's novel The Bird is a Raven. His trans-lation of The Essential Writings of Machiavelli was a finalist for the 2008 PEN/Book-of-the-Month Club Translation Prize.

Michel Delville teaches comparative literature at the University of Liège, Belgium. He is the author or co-author of ca. twenty books including The American Prose Poem; Food, Poetry, and the Aesthetics of Consumption: Eating the Avant-Garde; Crossroads Poetics; The Political Aes-

thetics of Hunger and Disgust (w. Andrew Norris); *Undoing Art* (w. Mary Ann Caws) and several prose poetry collections. His forthcoming publications include *The Edinburgh Companion to the Prose Poem* and *About the French Prose Poem* (New York Review Books), both co-edited with Mary Ann Caws.

John Hargraves is a former professor of German at Yale and Connecticut College. He has translated many German works into English, and has written a book on music and Hermann Broch and other writers. He is an active musician, and performs with a singing group at clubs in New York and elsewhere. He is also a member of the board of the Mac-Dowell Colony and the Metropolitan Opera Guild in New York, and Musical Masterworks in Old Lyme, CT.

James Huneker (1857–1921) was an American art, music, and literary critic. He was married to the painter and sculptor Clio Hinton Bracken. His work on Chopin was praised by Douglas Hofstadter, who playfully coined a unit for measuring a brain's quantity of soul a "huneker" in his 2007 essay "I Am A Strange Loop." Huneker's translation of Baudelaire's complete poems and poems in prose appeared in 1919.

John Irons studied French, German and Dutch at Cambridge. He subsequently did a doctorate on imagery in the poetry of a Dutch poet, P.C. Boutens. In 1968, he moved to Scandinavia, where he has lived ever since, mostly in Denmark, but also in Sweden. Alongside his career as a teacher at a university and, later, a college of education, he has been a professional translator since the mid-1980s. He has specialised in translating poetry and translates into English from Danish, Swedish and Norwegian as well as from the three languages studied earlier. He has a blogsite for his poetry translations that has been in existence for ten years. There is a more detailed CV at this blogsite (johnirons.blogspot.com).

M. Kasper is a book artist and translator, and a retired librarian. A revised, enlarged edition of Kasper's translation of the Lettrist Gabriel Pomerand's verbo-visual masterpiece, *Saint Ghetto of the Loans,* is due soon from Ugly Duckling Presse.

Rosemary Lloyd was educated at the University of Adelaide, where she is an affiliate professor, and Cambridge, where she taught, and is Rudy Professor Emerita at Indiana University. She specializes in nineteenth-century French poetry and painting, has translated a range of French poets and prose writers, and is the author of many books, including *Mallarmé: The Poet and His Circle, Baudelaire's World, The Land of Lost Content: Children and Childhood in Nineteenth-Century French Literature,* and *Shimmering in a Transformed Light: Writing the Still Life.* She has edited many volumes, including the *Cambridge Companion to Baudelaire, Revolutions in Writing: Readings in Nineteenth-century French Prose,* and *Women Seeking Expression: France 1789–1914.* In retirement much of her time is devoted to birdwatching.

Gian Lombardo's books include the prose poetry collections *Machines We Have Built* (2014), *Who Lets Go First* (2010), *Aid & A_Bet* (2008), *Of All the Corners to Forget* (2004), *Sky Open Again* (1997), *Before Arguable Answers* (1993), and *Standing Room* (1989) as well as the poetry collection *Between Islands* (1984). Lombardo's translations include Michel Delville's *Anything & Everything* (2016), Archestratos's *Gastrology or Life of Pleasure or Study of the Belly or Inquiry Into Dinner* (2009), Michel Delville's *Third Body* (2009), Eugène Savitzkaya's *Rules of Solitude* (2004), and Aloysius Bertrand's *Flemish School, Old Paris, & Night and Its Spells* (2000). He directs Quale Press, which mainly publishes prose poetry, and teaches publishing at Emerson College.

Scott Mehl is Assistant Professor of Japanese at Colgate University, where he teaches Japanese language, literature, and culture. He has published articles on modern Japanese poetry (in *Japan Review, Japanese Language and Literature,* and *Southeast Review of Asian Studies*) and on topics in comparative literature (in *Japanese Studies, Comparative Literature Studies,* and *Studia Metrica et Poetica*). His translations of Japanese poetry and criticism have appeared in print and online (including *Japan Forum, Monumenta Nipponica,* and *The Politics and Literature Debate in Postwar Japanese Criticism*). He is writing a book on form and translation in modern Japanese poetics.

Stuart Merrill (1863–1915) was an American poet who wrote in French and spent most of his life in Europe. His *Pastels in Prose* (1890) was the first anthology of French prose poetry published in English. In 1895, Merrill unsuccessfully launched a petition to Queen Victoria asking for Oscar Wilde's release from prison, pleading for clemency "in the name of art and humanity" (among the prominent French writers he had contacted, the archconservatives and traditionalists Maurice Barrès and Paul Bourget agreed to sign, whereas Emile Zola, the Goncourt and Alphonse Daudet refused). Merrill's wife, of whom very little is known, was memorably portrayed by his fellow Symbolist Jean Delville as "Mysteriosa" in his *Portrait of Mrs Stuart Merrill*.

Mark Polizzotti has translated more than fifty books from the French, including works by Gustave Flaubert, Patrick Modiano, Marguerite Duras, André Breton, and Raymond Roussel. A Chevalier de l'Ordre des Arts et des Lettres and the recipient of a 2016 American Academy of Arts & Letters Award for Literature, he is the author of eleven books, including *Revolution of the Mind: The Life of André Breton,* a finalist for the PEN/Martha Albrand Award for First Nonfiction; *Luis Buñuel's Los Olvidados; Bob Dylan: Highway 61 Revisited;* and *Sympathy for the Traitor: A Translation Manifesto.* His essays and reviews have appeared in the *New York Times, New Republic, Wall Street Journal, ARTnews, Apollo, The Nation, Parnassus, Partisan Review, Bookforum,* and elsewhere. He directs the publications program at The Metropolitan Museum of Art in New York.

Marianna Rosen is a writer, scholar, and translator from Russian and Italian. She was born and raised in Russia, where she studied philology and worked as a journalist, reporting for a prime-time weekly political commentary talk show, co-writing the show's script and text. Marianna wrote her first fiction story while reporting on the war in Chechnya. She is working on a collection of short stories titled *The Dislocated Guide to Moscow,* centering on mad and disturbed personalities in Moscow and St. Petersburg during the times that were similarly mad and disturbed— post-Soviet Russia in the late 80s and early 90s. Marianna is pursuing a Ph.D. at the CUNY Graduate Center, with research on Italian and Russian early 20th-century avant-garde, Russian trans-rationalist poets, and

Italian and Soviet film. She is an editor-in-chief of *Fine Art Globe;* her writing appeared in *Elle, The New York Observer, Moscow Times, Ptuich,* and *Fine Art Globe.* Marianna currently lives in Williamsburg, Brooklyn with her three imaginary friends and a book of Nietzsche catchphrases.

Richard Sieburth is a translator, essayist, editor, and literary scholar, an authority on French renaissance poetry, European romanticism, and literary modernism. He edited Ezra Pound for the Library of America and for New Directions, and has translated Nostradamus, Maurice Scève, Louise Labé, Friedrich Hölderlin, Georg Büchner, Walter Benjamin, Gershom Scholem, Charles Baudelaire, Stéphane Mallarmé, Henri Michaux, Antonin Artaud, Michel Leiris, Eugène Guillevic, and Jacques Darras. He is a *Chevalier dans l'ordre des palmes académiques,* Fellow of the American Academy of Arts and Sciences, and received an Annual Award in Letters from the American Academy of Arts in Letters in 2017. His forthcoming *Late Baudelaire* (Yale UP, 2020) has been supported by a Guggenheim Fellowship for Translation. He received the PEN/Book-of the Month Translation Prize in 2000 for his *Selected Writings of Gérard de Nerval* and his *A Certain Plume* (Michaux) received the 2019 PEN Prize for Poetry in Translation.

Jake Syersak is a poet, translator, and editor. He is author of the poetry collections *Mantic Compost* and *Yield Architecture.* He is also the translator of several works by Moroccan surrealist Mohammed Khaïr-Eddine, including the hybrid novel *Agadir* (co-translated with Pierre Joris) and the poetry collection *Proximal Morocco.*

Rosanna Warren is a poet, painter, and literary critic. She has taught at Vanderbilt University, Boston University, in several medium security prisons in Massachusetts, and is Hanna Holborn Gray Distinguished Service Professor in the Committee on Social Thought at the University of Chicago. Her *The Art of Translation: Voices from the Field* appeared in 1989, *Fables of the Self: Studies in Lyric Poetry* in 2008, and *Max Jacob: A Life in Art and Letters* in 2020. Her many books of poems include *So Forth* (2020), *Ghost in a Red Hat* (2011), and *Departure* (2003). She is the recipient of awards from the Academy of American Poets, The American

Academy of Arts & Letters, the Lila Wallace Foundation, the Guggenheim Foundation, the American Council of Learned Societies, and the New England Poetry Club, among others. She was a Chancellor of the Academy of American Poets from 1999 to 2005, and is a member of the American Academy of Arts and Letters, the American Academy of Arts and Sciences, and the American Philosophical Society.

Matvei Yankelevich is the managing editor and one of the founders of the Ugly Duckling Presse, where he edits the Eastern European Poets Series. His books and chapbooks include *Boris by the Sea* (Octopus Books), *The Present Work* (Palm Press), and *Writing in the Margin* (Loudmouth Collective). His translations from Russian have cropped up in *Calque, Circumference, Harpers, New American Writing, Poetry,* and the *New Yorker* and in some anthologies, including *OBERIU: An Anthology of Russian Absurdism* (Northwestern) and *Night Wraps the Sky: Writings by and about Mayakovsky* (FSG). His translations of Daniil Kharms were collected in *Today I Wrote Nothing: The Selected Writings of Daniil Kharms* (Ardis/ Overlook) He edited a portfolio of Contemporary Russian Poetry and Poetics for the magazine *Aufgabe* (No. 8, Fall 2009). He teaches at Hunter College, Columbia University School of the Arts (Writing Division), and the Milton Avery Graduate School of the Arts at Bard College.

BLACK WIDOW PRESS POETRY IN TRANSLATION

Sixty Years: Selected Poems 1957–2017 by Mikhail Yeryomin. Translated by J. Kates. *(forthcoming)*

Through Naked Branches by Tarjei Vesaas. Translated, edited, and introduced by Roger Greenwald.

To Speak, to Tell You? Poems by Sabine Sicaud. Translated by Norman R. Shapiro. Introduction and notes by Odile Ayral-Clause.

BLACK WIDOW PRESS
MODERN POETRY SERIES

WILLIS BARNSTONE
ABC of Translation
African Bestiary (forthcoming)

DAVE BRINKS
The Caveat Onus
The Secret Brain: Selected Poems 1995–2012

RUXANDRA CESEREANU
Crusader-Woman. Translated by Adam J. Sorkin. Introduction by Andrei Codrescu.
Forgiven Submarine by Ruxandra Cesereanu and Andrei Codrescu.

CLAYTON ESHLEMAN
An Alchemist with One Eye on Fire
Anticline
Archaic Design
Clayton Eshleman / The Essential Poetry: 1960–2015
Grindstone of Rapport: A Clayton Eshleman Reader
Penetralia
Pollen Aria
The Price of Experience
Endure: Poems by Bei Dao. Translated by Clayton Eshleman and Lucas Klein.
Curdled Skulls: Poems of Bernard Bador. Translated by Bernard Bador with Clayton Eshleman.

PIERRE JORIS
Barzakh (Poems 2000–2012)
Exile Is My Trade: A Habib Tengour Reader

MARILYN KALLET
How Our Bodies Learned
The Love That Moves Me
Packing Light: New and Selected Poems
Disenchanted City (La ville désenchantée) by Chantal Bizzini. Translated by J. Bradford Anderson, Darren Jackson, and Marilyn Kallet.

ROBERT KELLY
Fire Exit
The Hexagon

STEPHEN KESSLER
Garage Elegies
Last Call (forthcoming)

BILL LAVENDER
Memory Wing

HELLER LEVINSON
from stone this running
LinguaQuake
Lurk
Seep
Tenebraed
Un-
Wrack Lariat

JOHN OLSON
Backscatter: New and Selected Poems
Dada Budapest
Larynx Galaxy
Weave of the Dream King

NIYI OSUNDARE
City Without People: The Katrina Poems

MEBANE ROBERTSON
An American Unconscious
Signal from Draco: New and Selected Poems

JEROME ROTHENBERG
Concealments and Caprichos
Eye of Witness: A Jerome Rothenberg Reader. Edited with commentaries by Heriberto Yepez & Jerome Rothenberg.
The President of Desolation & Other Poems

AMINA SAÏD
The Present Tense of the World: Poems 2000–2009. Translated with an introduction by Marilyn Hacker.

ANIS SHIVANI
Soraya (Sonnets)

JERRY W. WARD, JR.
Fractal Song

BLACK WIDOW PRESS
ANTHOLOGIES / BIOGRAPHIES

Barbaric Vast & Wild: A Gathering of Outside and Subterranean Poetry (Poems for the Millennium, vol. 5). Jerome Rothenberg and John Bloomberg-Rissman, eds.

Clayton Eshleman: The Whole Art by Stuart Kendall

Revolution of the Mind: The Life of André Breton by Mark Polizzotti

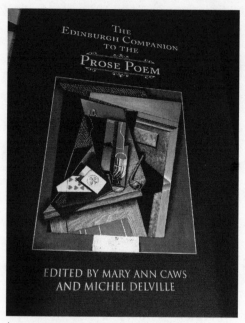

***The Edinburgh Companion to
the Prose Poem***
Edited by Mary Ann Caws and
Michel Delville
A collection of original essays
providing critical, international and
cross-disciplinary approaches to the
prose poem
• Provides the first international and
comparative approach to the prose
poem
• Includes chapters on non-Western
avatars of the genre
• Covers the history of the prose
poem from Baudelaire to our times

https://edinburghuniversitypress.com
/book/9781474462747